Helen has had a passion for cooking from an early age and the first recipe she tore out of a magazine was in '68 when she was 8 years old. She has kept a record of all the meals she has planned and cooked for over 40 years. As well as having a successful professional career, Helen has had a busy and sometimes challenging life story. She lives in Kent with her husband, Marc.

THE GO-TO COOKBOOK

Helen Hume

AUSTIN MACAULEY PUBLISHERS™
LONDON • CAMBRIDGE • NEW YORK • SHARJAH

A CIP catalogue record for this title is available from the British Library.

ISBN 9781398414709 (Paperback)
ISBN 9781398407749 (Hardback)
ISBN 9781398449329 (ePub e-book)

www.austinmacauley.com

First Published (2021)
Austin Macauley Publishers Ltd
25 Canada Square
Canary Wharf
London
E14 5LQ

For Holly, Rosie and Jack with lots of love from Granny
and in memory of Vicki, whom I miss every day.

A big thank you to all my family and friends who have eaten my food, asked for recipes over the years and inspired the idea for this book. A big thank you to Claire Hume for being my initial proofreader, food styling assistant and very efficient gofer. With gratitude to Lucy Richards for the brilliant artistic photographs, it was such a pleasure working with you. To Amy Kinnear for all the food styling advice and encouragement and to Joe Russell, a great and generous sub-editor, for making sure the recipes make sense. A special mention to Cathy and Vernon Hull. It was Vernon and Marc who decided this book should be published and Cathy who supported me through the process. To Rebecca for being a wonderful daughter in every way and giving me grandchildren. Holly, Rosie and Jack are a joy in my life and this book is for them so they can cook as adults and think of Granny. Finally to the main man, my husband Marc, who is my biggest champion and a happy eater; thank you for all your love and support.

Table of Contents

1. Introduction   9

2. Why Plan Ahead?   12

3. My Life in the Kitchen 1979–Early 80s   16

Brunch and Lunch   18

4. My Life in the Kitchen 1982–1990   38

Easy Everyday   41

5. My Life in the Kitchen 1990–2000   89

Feeding Friends / Entertaining   94

6. My Life in the Kitchen 2000–2010   131

Sweet Things   134

7. My Life in the Kitchen 2010–2020   166

Baking   169

8. Index Recipe notes   200

1. Introduction
My Life in the Kitchen

Cooking has provided an evolving narrative to my life. I have kept a detailed record of all the meals I have cooked for some 40 years, along with recipes upon which they are based. Culled from the widest range of sources, – magazines and newspapers to cookery books from around the world – I have worked and reworked these recipes according to my preferences, my family's likes and dislikes and the reaction of my guests. 'I would really love the recipe for that,' is the comment that often follows one of my suppers. Invariably, this will be a recipe that has evolved over the years from something torn out or copied on a scrap of paper that I have kept in my now voluminous collection. It always brings me great pleasure in sharing recipes and knowing that some will be passed on through other families.

So many people have said to me that I should share some of my favourite tried and tested recipes by bringing them together in one book. In doing so, I hope that it will provide a useful resource for those leading the kind of busy life I have and want some simple and practical ways to create good and healthy food every day of the week. But also, I hope it will provide an insight into the ways our culinary tastes have changed over the years, reflecting such factors as the growing influence of world cuisine, celebrity and TV chefs, and the increased emphasis on healthy eating.

Let me tell you a little bit more about me and my life in the kitchen. Some of my earliest memories are of baking a trays of fairy cakes – decorating each one with white icing, glace cherries and angelica. Another memory is of making Christmas coconut ice, colouring one half a deep pink and keeping the other as white as snow. I must have been reasonably competent as in 1971, aged 12, I won first prize at the Local Horticultural Society Show for my decorated cupcakes. Today, I have three grandchildren and they, too, are slowly, under Granny's watchful eye, discovering recipes and getting their hands sticky! But for me, cooking has always meant more than simply having fun. It is through good food that I bring family and friends together. Surely, there is nothing better than people huddled around the kitchen table sharing stories and eating! Food has also given me strength in coping with traumatic times in my life. When Vicki, my youngest daughter, became terminally ill, cooking her favourite food was one of the many ways in which I was able to care for her and show her love.

Although my interest is in adapting rather than creating my own recipes, in 1973 I won a commendation in a Daily Mirror Children's literacy competition for my recipe for a teacher. I used to spend hours poring over my mother's collection of Cordon Bleu magazines, but it was not until 1974 that I had a cookery book of my own. My father bought me my first much loved recipe book, The Cookery Year by Reader's Digest. This publication gave background to all sorts of techniques as well as seasonal eating. The family came to appreciate the book because I would cook the Apple Strudel recipe regularly for Sunday dessert. The recipe instruction for the filo pastry is that it should be stretched 'thin enough to read a love letter through'. This romantic notion kept me occupied for hours before filo pastry became widely available to buy.

Since leaving school I have taken several post-graduate qualifications, including an MA in Business Management but apart from my O Level in Domestic Science,

I have never taken a qualification in food. I chose the subject because I had an interest in food. My teacher felt it was a useful subject because good cooking 'was the way to a man's heart'! I have had a professional career whilst raising two children – Rebecca and Vicki, so I know how hard it is to juggle work and home as well as preparing nutritious scrumptious food. Therefore, in this book, I have included easy and simple family supper recipes, as well as those for entertaining when you may have more time to create something special. I have also explored the secret to good cooking every day, it lies in planning ahead!

I now have over 40 years of records of what I have cooked and eaten both on a day-to-day basis and when entertaining. Looking back, it is evident that my food tastes have changed. I bought my first vegetarian cookbook in 1986 but changing the family diet to more plant based was a very uphill struggle with three committed 'meatatarians'. In 40 years, availability of food has changed as has our knowledge of diet. However, recipes do endure, I am still using recipes from 50 years ago and as my first dinner party illustrates, the avocado was not invented in the twenty-first century.

I have been influenced by many twentieth-century cookery writers and chefs. I still rely on Delia to help me cook Christmas lunch. Influences have come from Mary Berry, Raymond Blanc, Nigel Slater, Gordon Ramsay and in the last few years, Yotom Ottolengi. I was an avid reader of Good Housekeeping when I was first married nearly 40 years ago and even appeared in one edition in a fashion feature.

I was motivated to write this book as a legacy for my three grandchildren, but over the years I am constantly asked to share recipes and suggest recipe ideas. Therefore, the idea to create a book for all was born. It has been a challenge to choose which recipes to include but the book is an illustration of how my husband, Marc, and I eat now whilst reflecting that many recipes and ingredients endure, it is just life that has changed.

2. Why Plan Ahead?

For those not used to the concept it can seem a time-consuming chore. Believe me, once you start planning you will never go shopping again without a list. You will never look in your fridge when you get home from work for supper inspiration, you will have the pleasure of looking forward to a tasty supper that you have already planned and shopped for.

Saves money– you do not buy ingredients you are not planning to use.

Saves waste– you buy what you intend to cook and eat. You plan to use ingredients you have not used in the previous week due to changes in your plans. You plan to use leftovers.

Saves time – you plan to cook ahead for quick easy meals in minutes. You create a shopping list which makes shopping in a supermarket or online quicker and easier. You will only need to shop once a week and no impulse buying 'just in case' food. Planning ensures you have ingredients to hand when you need them, no last-minute dash to the shops.

Ensures variety and balance– you will not end up eating pasta every night. You can plan a balanced diet with plenty of vegetables and fruit. It enables you to plan seasonal eating and to eat a range of food groups.

How to plan:

• Think about the meals your family love to eat and those you cook regularly, most people have a few signature dishes that the family love whether it is chicken curry, Shepherd's pie or macaroni cheese. Make a list of these meals, include seasonal favourites. Use these meals as a basis for your planning and then aim to introduce a couple of new recipes a week. Inspiration can come from recipes you have collected, recipe books or online. These new recipes may become family favourites of the future.

• Use an exercise book, kitchen diary or online app and plan your meals 1–2 weeks in advance.

• Look at your family calendar and note how many you are cooking for, which days you will have very little time and those days you will have more time. I tend to plan every evening meal and weekend lunches.

• Plan to use leftovers and days when you are planning to have a takeaway or eat out. Write your shopping list around the ingredients you need, checking your store cupboard and fridge.

• If your plans change, swap your menus around and use the ingredients that will go out of date first. This is a flexible plan to make your life easier. Find a system of meal planning that works for you.

• Batch cook occasionally, for example, tomato sauce in the freezer can form the basis of lots of quick, easy and nutritious meals.

3. My Life in the Kitchen 1979–Early 80s

I was only 20 in October 1979 when I married Martin. My Domestic Science O level had trained me to plan meals so it seemed sensible to write down what we would eat every evening. This was to enable me to create a shopping list, avoid waste and save money. I returned from honeymoon and cooked my first meal of roast beef, roast potatoes and parsnips, swede and cauliflower, followed by lemon steamed pudding. I was working full-time but would come home every evening to cook a very meat-based meal and a pudding. Our first dinner party was a few weeks later in early 1980. I could have cooked the same meal today and I am not sure anyone would think it to be an 80s revival meal. We ate avocado with French dressing, beef Stroganoff rice, French beans, followed by chocolate mousse and oranges in caramel.

We lived in an old house that needed lots of renovation so working full-time, providing a meal every night was a challenge to a young wife who had just left home. My skills were to be stretched further when we ripped the old kitchen out and it took us three months to replace it. This was an era before microwaves, so everything was cooked on a two-ring burner mainly in a pressure cooker. In 1979, we did not have many kitchen gadgets, but I was given a Magimix food processor (only available since 1974). It is still my must have bit of kit and the only thing on my kitchen worktop.

This was the era of buying half a lamb or pig for the freezer, then planning meals around how to eat all the bits of meat. Sunday was always a roast and Monday was often cold meat with baked potatoes. My nod to vegetarianism was macaroni cheese or quiche. At this time, I was partial to Angel Delight and would happily whisk some up if I was in a hurry.

It was during this time I met my first vegetarian; the only problem was she told me as she sat down to supper. A memorable guest because she also insisted on smoking between courses, unthinkable today – they did not get another invite!

Example weekly menus from 1979 - early 1980's

Sunday
Roast pork/roast potatoes/carrots/brussels
Apple crunch

Monday
Pork loaf/baked potatoes/peas
Treacle tart/cream

Tuesday
Devilled kidneys/rice
Baked apple

Wednesday
Chilli con carne/rice
Chocolate mousse (recipe page 142)

Thursday
Toad in the hole/peas/carrots
Steamed pudding/custard

Friday
Keema curry
Crème caramel

Saturday, 18 October 1980
Avocado pear with prawns
Pigeon stuffed with pate
Baked potatoes
Green beans in sour cream/carrots
Oranges in caramel/brandy snaps (recipe page 160)
Apple strudel (recipe page 144)

Brunch and Lunch

Granola

I first started making granola in 1994 when it was more unusual than it is today. I must have been asked for the recipe more times than any other. Marc has created his own lunchtime pudding using plain yoghurt with a spoonful of jam topped with granola. Most people would eat this at breakfast but sometimes as a quick snack it is hard to resist.

Makes approx. fifteen 75 g servings

425 g jumbo oats
110 g desiccated coconut
200 g flaked almonds
50 g sunflower seeds
100 g pumpkin seeds
250 g runny honey

1.   Preheat the oven to fan 180/200/gas 6.
2.   Combine all the ingredients in a large bowl and transfer to two large roasting tins.
3.   Place in the oven for ten minutes. Remove and stir. Return to the oven for a further five minutes, remove and stir again. The nuts and oats should be toasted golden, but you don't want to burn them. If needed, the granola may need a few extra minutes, but remember to set your timer as it will quickly go from golden to burnt.
4.   Once cool, store in an airtight container.

I am not a fan of dried fruit in granola or muesli, but once the granola has cooled, you can add any 200 g of dried fruit of your choice. Serve with milk or plain yoghurt with fresh fruit on top. When in season this works well with poached forced rhubarb and yoghurt.

Bircher Muesli

We discovered the delights of Bircher muesli when we were on honeymoon in the Maldives. This recipe is always served at breakfast to anyone who stays overnight; everyone loves it. It makes for a great breakfast on the move – there have been many times when we have eaten it in the Channel Tunnel.

Serves 4-6

200 g rolled oats
350 ml apple juice
1 dessert apple
125 g Greek yoghurt
100 g granola
Blueberries to serve

1. Place the oats and apple juice in a bowl and leave overnight in the fridge.
2. Before serving, remove the core from the apple and grate into the oats. Stir in yoghurt and granola. (You may wish to add more yoghurt if the mixture is too thick.)
3. Serve the Bircher muesli with berries or any other seasonal fruit of your choice.

Sweet Seville Orange Marmalade

We do eat rather a lot of marmalade and in the interests of both taste and cost it makes sense to make it. Seville oranges are available for about a month starting just after the New Year, so on a cold wet day, why not fill your house with the aroma of oranges and make some? I have tried lots of recipes over the years and this is by far the easiest way to make marmalade, especially if like me you are trying to make a year's supply.

Makes enough for 7-8 jars

700 g Seville oranges
4½ pints water
2 kg sugar
Juice from 1½ lemons

1.   Wash and halve the oranges. Remove and reserve the pips, place the pips in piece of muslin and tie securely.
2.   Quarter the oranges and blitz in a food processor until they are in small chunks. Do not process to a paste or you will lose the texture of the marmalade.
3.   Place in a large bowl with the bag of pips. Cover with the water and leave overnight.
4.   In a very large lidded pan simmer the fruit for 1½ hours until the peel is soft. Place a tea plate in the fridge for testing later.
5.   Wash jam jars in hot water and place in a warm oven 140°C for ten minutes to sterilise them.
6.   Remove the lid from the pan and the bag of pips, add the sugar and lemon juice. Stir over a medium heat until the sugar has dissolved.
7.   Raise the heat to its highest and boil rapidly until the marmalade has set. The setting point is likely to be reached after about 20 minutes. To test, remove the pan from the heat, place a small spoonful of the marmalade on the chilled plate, return to fridge and leave for one minute. Push your finger across it – if you see it wrinkle, you have reached setting point. (If it is not ready, return the pan to the boil and test again a few minutes later.)
8.   Once ready, stir to reduce the temperature slightly and pour into the warm jars. Cover with waxed discs and seal with jam pot covers. Once cold, place the jam jar lids on.

Wheaten Bread

Often known as Irish soda bread, this recipe for wheaten bread was given to me by my friend, Jo, who was given it by her Irish mother-in-law. It is a great base for a smoked salmon canapé or lightly toasted then topped with crushed avocado and smoked salmon, or just butter and jam.

Makes 1 loaf

60 g butter
225 g wholemeal flour
140 g plain four
1 tsp sugar
1 tsp bicarbonate of soda
1 tsp salt
300 ml buttermilk (or 150 ml milk with 150 ml runny natural yoghurt)

1.   Preheat the oven to 180 fan/200/gas 6.
2.   Rub the butter into the flours then add the other dry ingredients. Mix well.
3.   Add the buttermilk and stir into the flour mix to form a sticky dough. Turn onto a lightly floured surface and form a loaf shape – don't knead it or you will make the dough heavy. Place in a small grease loaf tin then bake for about 40 minutes, until the bread sounds hollow when tapped on the base. If the bread is not ready, return to the oven upside down and bake for a few more minutes.

This shape makes it easier to slice for canapés. The more traditional shape is to make a ball shape of about 18 cm diameter and make a shallow cross on the top with a knife.

Leek and Cannellini Bean Soup

If you do not have a tin of cannellini beans you can substitute with butter beans.

Serves 4

2 leeks
1 tbsp olive oil
15 g butter
1 crushed clove of garlic
2 large floury potatoes (approx. 300 g), diced
1½ pints of vegetable stock
1 x 410 g can of cannellini beans, drained and rinsed
1 bay leaf
15 g chopped flat leaf parsley
salt and freshly ground black pepper

1.   Halve the leeks, wash well and thinly slice.
2.   Heat the oil and butter and sweat the leeks over a low heat until soft but not coloured, for approx. ten minutes. Add the garlic and potatoes and stir for a further two minutes.
3.   Add the stock, beans, bay leaf and half the parsley. Bring to the boil then cover and simmer very gently for 20 minutes. Stir in the remaining parsley. Season and serve.

Squash and Sweet Potato Soup

Soup is so quick easy and nutritious. In 15 minutes, you can have a pot of soup simmering away and a quick blitz half an hour later and you have a great lunch. If you want to make it more substantial serve with grated cheese and croutons or just crusty French bread. Soups also make great starters.

Serves 6-8

1 tbsp olive oil
1 large white onion
750 g butternut squash, peeled and chopped
2 sweet potatoes, peeled and chopped
2tsp ground coriander
½ tsp chilli flakes
2½ pints of vegetable stock
chilli oil to serve (optional)

1.	Heat the oil and fry the onion over a low heat until soft but not coloured, approx. ten minutes. Add the spices and cook for a further two minutes.
2.	Add the squash and the potatoes and cook for five minutes. Add the stock, bring to the boil and simmer very gently for 30 minutes.
3.	Whiz the soup, a stick blender is perfect for this. Check the seasoning and serve with a drizzle of chilli oil.

Tomato Soup

I have been making tomato soup for lunch since I was in my teens. We would use tinned tomatoes and flour to thicken, far superior to the Heinz version most people ate at the time. This version uses butter beans for a thicker consistency, which also improves the nutritional content.

Serves 4

1 tbsp olive oil
1 onion, chopped
2 x 400 g tin tomatoes
70 g double concentrate tomato puree
2 x 400 g tin butter beans drained
1pint vegetable stock
salt and black pepper

1.   Heat the oil in a large saucepan set over a low heat. Fry the onion for ten minutes until soft but not coloured.
2.   Add the tomatoes, tomato puree, butter beans and stock. Cover the pan and simmer very gently for 20 minutes. Blitz the soup until smooth, season to taste then serve.

Avocado and Orange Salad

I love avocado, and orange cuts through its richness. I've been serving avocado since 1970s, though it used to be in specially shaped dishes with French dressing poured into the centre. This recipe can be a quick light lunch, starter or side salad.

Serves 6 as a starter or 4 as a light lunch

50 g pumpkin seeds
2 large oranges
2 ripe avocados
4 tbsp olive oil
2 tsp Dijon mustard
pinch of caster sugar
100 g watercress

1.   To toast the pumpkin seeds, wipe a frying pan with a very small amount of oil and place over a medium heat. Add the pumpkin seeds, sprinkle lightly with sea salt and stir until they are toasted and starting to turn brown.
2.   Peel the oranges and cut into segments by cutting between the membrane to segment the orange. Reserve the juice. Peel the avocados, remove the stone and cut into chunks or slices.
3.   Whisk the oil, mustard, two tbsp of the orange juice and the sugar together. Season.
4.   Divide the watercress among plates, place the orange and avocado on top, drizzle over the dressing and sprinkle with the pumpkin seeds.

Hot Tomato Salad on Sourdough Toast

When I first made this 25 years ago, I made it as a starter. It is so easy that I now also make it for a quick lunch.

Serves 6 as a starter

750 g mixed cherry tomatoes (red and yellow)
2 tbsp capers, drained
1tsp caster sugar
100 ml olive oil
salt and black pepper
6 thick slices of sourdough bread
fresh basil
thick balsamic vinegar

1.   Pre heat the oven 180 fan/200/gas 6.
2.   Halve the cherry tomatoes and place in a roasting tin with all but two tbsp of the oil, all the sugar, capers and seasoning. Place the bread on a separate baking tray, drizzle with remaining oil and season.
3.   Place the tomatoes and bread in the oven for ten minutes until the bread is golden and the tomatoes have softened and are hot.
4.   Place the bread on serving plates and top with tomatoes. Sprinkle with basil and drizzle with a few drops of balsamic vinegar. Serve hot.

Pear, Watercress and Roquefort Salad

This recipe can be a quick light lunch, starter or side salad

Serves 6 as a starter or 4 as a light lunch

juice of ½lemon
5 tbsp hazelnut oil
1 tbsp red wine vinegar
200 g watercress, washed and dried
3 ripe dessert pears such as Rocha or Williams
250 g Roquefort (or any blue cheese)
150 g toasted hazelnuts, coarsely chopped
salt and black pepper

1.   Make the dressing by mixing the lemon juice, oil and vinegar. Season
to taste.
2.   Remove any woody stems from the watercress and divide between plates.
3.   Core and thinly slice the pears, then arrange over the watercress.
4.   Crumble over the Roquefort cheese, sprinkle with the hazelnuts and drizzle
with the dressing. Serve.
To toast the nuts, place in a roasting tin and toast for about 15 minutes in a
preheated oven, 160 fan/180/gas 4. Check after 10 minutes as they will
burn easily.

Gorgonzola, Chicory and Walnut Salad

This recipe can be a quick light lunch, starter or side salad.

Serves 4 as a starter

2 heads of chicory red or white
1 crisp dessert apple
75 g gorgonzola
100 g walnuts, roughly chopped
1 celery stick, thinly sliced

For the dressing:

1 tbsp Dijon mustard
2 tbsp water
2 tbsp walnut oil
2 tbsp olive oil
1 tbsp white wine vinegar
salt and black pepper

1.   Make the dressing by mixing the mustard with the water before adding the oils and vinegar. Whisk vigorously to emulsify then season to taste.
2.   Cut the base off the chicory and peel off the leaves until you get to the centre. Cut the centre into quarters. Core the apple and thinly slice.
3.   Divide the chicory and apple among the plates. Crumble over the cheese and scatter over the walnuts and celery. Pour over the dressing and serve.

Gorgonzola, Chicory and Fig Salad

A variation on Gorgonzola, chicory and walnut salad, replace the celery and apple with four quartered figs.
Add one tsp of honey to the dressing.

Warm Asparagus and Rocket Salad with Pesto Dressing

I have been making this for 16 years and as the asparagus season is quite short it is always a treat in April. We are lucky enough to have an asparagus farm close to us and for about eight weeks of the year we eat rather a lot of asparagus. This makes a great lunch or starter.

Serves 6 as a starter or 4 as a light lunch

200 g small new potatoes
3 tbsp pesto
2 tsp olive oil
2 tsp lemon juice
500 g asparagus
50 g rocket leaves
Parmesan shavings to serve

1.   Boil the new potatoes until tender. Drain and set aside.
2.   Mix the pesto, olive oil and lemon juice. Season to taste.
3.   For the asparagus, snap the stems and discard the woody end. Cook in a pan of boiling water for three minutes until just tender. Drain.
4.   To serve, divide the rocket among plates and arrange the potatoes and asparagus on top. Drizzle with the dressing and scatter with parmesan shavings.

Beetroot and Orange Pate

My childhood memories of beetroot were the pickled variety and I hated the way the pink vinegary juice seeped across the plate. This recipe has restored my faith in the humble beetroot. I used this recipe in a magazine article I appeared in with Holly and Rosie. The article was 'Tea with Granny', and this is such a pretty colour that it appeals to children, but you may have to tone down the horseradish. The texture is more like a stiff hummus than a pate.

Serves 4-6

450 g fresh beetroot
1 tbsp olive oil
1 tsp ground cumin
juice and zest of 1 small orange
200 g full fat cream cheese
hot horseradish sauce to taste (approx. 1 tbsp)
1 tbsp Greek yogurt mixed with horseradish sauce to taste (optional topping)

1.   Preheat the oven to 180 fan/200/gas 6.
2.   Peel the beetroot and cut into even sized 2 cm chunks. Coat in the oil and cumin and transfer to a roasting tray. Cook for 30 minutes until tender. Cool slightly.
3.   Blitz in a food processor with the orange zest and juice, cream cheese and horseradish until smooth. Check seasoning and transfer to a serving bowl.
4.   Serve with pitta bread, bread stick or crudities such as carrot batons and celery.

If serving on Bruchetta, top with a small amount of Greek yoghurt topping and finish with orange zest.

4. My Life in the Kitchen
1982–1990

I seemed to spend a lot of time in the 1980s making cakes, wedding cakes for friends, christening cakes for family and lots of children's birthday cake. Rebecca and I share a birthday and I would often spend hours the day before my birthday, fighting with cake and butter cream trying to replicate a fairy castle or a 'My Little Pony'. I bought my first vegetarian cookery book in 1986 and can see from my records that I started to introduce nut roasts and vegetarian hot pots into my weekly menus. My main recipe influences were still coming from Good Housekeeping magazine, but I did see a Mary Berry cookery demonstration during this time and bought a couple of her books, Farmhouse Cooking was a favourite. I was still making a pudding most evenings, but they tended to be getting lighter and more fruit based over the decade.

We continued to entertain on a regular basis usually 20 to 25 times a year, but we only went out to eat three times a year on birthdays and wedding anniversary. No wonder it seemed like a busy decade. My first daughter Rebecca was born in 1982 and Vicki in 1985. We moved first in 1983 to a larger house with a kitchen/breakfast room overlooking a big garden. The only downside was the whole kitchen ceiling, walls and units were pine, it was like cooking in a sauna, but I did have a rather old built-in cooker and a separate hob which seemed the height of sophistication to me. Kitchen gadgets were coming onto the market thick and fast at this time. Martin was a product development manager at Black and Decker so I would get to try all manner of gadgets such as coffee machines, deep fat fryers and electric woks. Not wanting to clutter up the kitchen and finding I could manage quite happily without them, none of them became a permanent acquisition. However, I did discover the stick blender which makes liquidising soup a cinch, and I have one in the kitchen to this day.

In 1987, we moved 300 miles away to Hexham, far from family and friends, the upside was a brand-new kitchen in a new house and a great fresh fish shop in the town. Unfortunately, the nearest Sainsbury's was 25 miles away and the nearest Waitrose, which had been my go-to store in Windsor, was over 200 miles away! We had lots of family and friends to stay and it is in this time that I learnt how to be a good guest – not everyone is!

Example weekly menus from 1980's

Sunday
Roast beef, Yorkshire pudding, roast potatoes, carrots, broccoli
Key lime pie

Monday
Khichri (recipe page 71)
Pineapple pudding

Tuesday
Stuffed courgettes, new potatoes
Blackcurrant fluff

Wednesday
Salmon and watercress roll, potatoes and peas
Fruit salad

Thursday
Pork chops with peanut sauce, rice
Banana and grape brûlée

Friday
Smoked mackerel and orange kebabs, green salad
Spiced Muscovado swirl

Saturday,20 May 1989–*Helen's 30th Birthday Party for 60*
Curried Turkey, Tuna eggs, Blue cheese quiche
West coast salad, spicy brown rice salad, bean salad, tomato salad, mushroom salad, new potatoes with watercress.
Garlic Bread
Chocolate bavarois
Strawberries and cream
Hazelnut vacherin (recipe page 135)
Cheesecake

Easy Everyday

The Most Useful Easy Tomato Sauce

One of my favourite meals as a child was a 'Women and Home' recipe for grilled sausages on a bed of noodles covered in tomato sauce and topped grated cheddar before being grilled until golden. I no longer eat sausages, but I still love pasta and tomato sauce.

I make this recipe in bulk and freeze into portions that will feed two. The sauce is great on its own with pasta but can form the basis of several supper dishes. Kids love this sauce, too, so I add seasoning depending on who I'm serving it to.

3 tbsp olive oil
750 g chopped onions
5 x 400 g cans of tomatoes (the best quality you can afford   – they are tastier)
140 g tomato puree
4 tsp dried oregano

1.   Heat the oil in a large saucepan set over a low heat. Fry the onion for ten minutes until soft but not coloured.
2.   Add all the other ingredients, cover the pan and simmer on a low heat for 1½ hours, stirring occasionally, until thick.
3.   Leave to cool then blend until smooth. Divide the sauce into 400 g portions and freeze.

This recipe forms the basis for:

- *Aubergines Imam Bayıldı*
- *Gnocchi with tomato and basil sauce*
- *No stir tomato and basil risotto*
- *Puttanesca pasta*
- *Easy veggie lasagne*

Tarts Spaghetti

I first heard of puttanesca pasta when Delia introduced it in her summer recipe book in 1993. I loved it but had to develop an anchovy-free version because Marc hates anchovies.

Serves 4
400 g spaghetti
100 g pitted dry black olives (if you find these too strong use any black olives)
2 x 400 g portions easy tomato sauce (page 42)
3 tbsp capers, drained
1 bunch of fresh basil, chopped
½ tsp dried chilli
Salt and black pepper
Grated parmesan, to serve

1.   Cook the spaghetti in a large pan of boiling water according to pack instructions.
2.   Meanwhile, roughly chop the black olives and combine with the tomato sauce, capers, basil, chilli flakes and seasoning.
3.   Drain the spaghetti and add to the sauce. Return to the heat for a few minutes and stir until the sauce is warm. Serve at once in warm bowls then grate with parmesan.

Aubergines Iman Bayıldı

Although this recipe is Turkish in origin, this is a simple un-spiced version and I serve it with baked potato, green beans and a good dollop of Greek yoghurt.

Serves 6

6 aubergine
Olive oil
2 x 400 g portions of easy tomato sauce (page 42)
½ bunch flat leaf parsley
Salt and black pepper

1.   Preheat the oven to fan 160/180/ gas 4. Halve the aubergines and score a criss-cross pattern across the cut side, making sure you do not cut all the way through. Heat olive oil in a frying pan and in two batches, fry the aubergines on all sides until golden.
2.   Place snugly in an ovenproof serving dish and spoon over the tomato sauce. Add three tbsp water to the dish and cover with foil. Bake for one hour.
3.   Sprinkle with parsley. The Imam Bayıldı can be served hot or it can be made in advance and served at room temperature.

Quick Veggie Lasagne

Yet another way to use the easy tomato sauce and although it takes 40 minutes to cook, it only takes minutes to put together.

Serves 6

400 g easy tomato sauce (page 42)
1 x 400 g tin of Puy lentils
50 g pitted dry black olives
2 tbsp capers, drained
zest of 1 lemon
pinch of dried chilli
½ bunch basil, chopped
salt and black pepper
250 g mozzarella
250 g dried lasagne sheets
Olive oil

1.   Preheat the oven to 180 fan/200/gas 6.
2.   Mix together the tomato sauce, lentils, olives, capers, lemon zest, chilli, basil and seasoning.
3.   Spoon ⅓ of the sauce into an ovenproof dish, approx. 20 cm x 30 cm. Tear over ⅓ of the mozzarella then cover with a layer of lasagna sheets. Repeat for another two layers finishing with the final third of the sauce topped with the remaining mozzarella.
4.   Drizzle with olive oil and bake for 30 to 40 minutes until the mozzarella is golden and the lasagna is bubbling. Serve with a green salad.

No-Stir Basil and Tomato Risotto

A risotto is always an easy supper but stirring all the time means you are rather tied to the stove. This recipe omits the need to stand and stir and it still has a great texture.

Serves 4

10g of fresh basil, chopped
knob of butter
1 tbsp olive oil
1 small red onion, finely chopped
400 g risotto rice
400 g easy tomato sauce (page 42)
150 ml white wine
600 ml hot vegetable stock
75 g cream cheese
50 g grated parmesan
Salt and black pepper

1.   In a large pan, sauté the onion in the butter and oil until soft. Add the rice and stir for one minute before adding the wine. Cook until the rice absorbs the wine.
2.   Stir in the tomato sauce and stock, reduce the heat to low and cover the risotto. Cook for 20 minutes, until the rice is tender, and the liquid has been absorbed.
3.   Stir in the cream cheese, basil and seasoning. Leave to stand for a few minutes before serving with parmesan.

Gnocchi with Tomato Sauce

This recipe first appears in my diary records in 2003 and has featured on a regular basis since. The sort of godsend recipe after a busy day and little time to cook supper.
This recipe serves two very generously but with the delicious creamy sauce it is not hard to eat it all. If you do not have Gruyère cheese to hand, cheddar works perfectly well.

Serves 2

1 x 400 g portion of easy tomato sauce (page 42)
150 ml whipping cream
1 x 500 g pack gnocchi
Chopped 1/2 bunch of fresh basil
50 g grated Gruyère cheese
salt and black pepper

1.   Place the tomato sauce and cream in a pan. Season and simmer without a lid for 15 minutes until thickened.
2.   Cook the gnocchi in a large pan of salted water according to the instructions. Drain and put in an ovenproof shallow serving dish. Stir in all the tomato sauce and half the basil then sprinkle grated cheese on top.
3.   Pop under a preheated grill for a few minutes until bubbling and the cheese is starting to turn brown.
4.   Serve in warm bowls with the remaining basil scatted on top.

Avocado and Pistachio Spaghetti

In the 1980s, I would make an avocado risotto, but much prefer this pasta avocado recipe. This can be made in the time the spaghetti takes to cook.

Serves 4

400 g spaghetti
grated zest of 1 lemon and juice of ½
2 ripe avocados
4 tbsp drained capers
bunch of fresh basil
75 g pistachio nuts, coarsely chopped
Olive oil
salt and black pepper
grated parmesan to serve (optional)

1.   Cook the pasta in a large pan of boiling water according to the instructions.
2.   Meanwhile, zest and juice the lemon. Peel the avocados, remove the stones and cut the flesh into cubes. Roughly chop the basil and chop the nuts.
3.   Drain the pasta and return to the pan. Add the lemon zest and juice, pistachios, capers, basil and avocado. Season, add a glug of olive oil and stir together.
4.   Serve in warm bowls with grated parmesan if using.

Gingered Chicken with Noodles

I used to make this for my children's supper on a very regular basis. It was quick, easy, nutritious and more importantly they both liked it, which was pretty rare!

Serves 4

1 leek
1-inch piece fresh ginger
300 g skinless chicken breast fillet
1 tbsp oil
2 level tbsp mild curry paste
300 ml vegetable or chicken stock
300 ml coconut milk
Salt and black pepper
125 g egg noodles
2 tsp lemon juice

1.   Wash and thinly slice the leek, peel and grate the ginger and cut the chicken into bite-sized pieces.
2.   Heat the oil in a large non-stick pan and gently fry the leek and ginger until softened but not coloured.
3.   Add the chicken and curry paste and cook for a further three minutes. Stir in the stock, coconut milk and seasoning.
4.   Bring to the boil. Break the noodles in half and add to the pan. Cover and simmer for ten minutes or until the noodles are just tender, stirring occasionally and adding more stock if required.
5.   Add lemon juice and season to taste. Serve immediately.

Roasted Vegetables with Halloumi

I make this recipe regularly and will even make it when we go on self-catering holidays as it is so quick and easy to prepare. Even Marc has been known to make this and his culinary skills usually stop at toast! I have given a sausage version as well which pleases meat eaters.

Serves 4

600 g sweet potato
600 g red potato
1 red pepper
1 yellow pepper
400 g red onion
2 x 250 g halloumi
4 tbsp olive oil
salt and black pepper

1.   Preheat the oven to 220/fan 200/gas 7.
2.   Cut the vegetables into equally sized large chunks. Place in a bowl, coat in olive oil and season. Arrange on a large baking tray lined with baking parchment and then roast for 25 minutes. Turn the vegetables and return to the oven for a further 15 minutes.
3.   Cut the halloumi into 16 slices and place on top of the vegetables. Return to the oven for 10 to 15 minutes until the halloumi has started to brown. Serve immediately with green vegetables of your choice.

Roasted Vegetables with Sausages, Horseradish Sauce and Baby Yorkshires

Serves 4

600 g sweet potato
600 g red potato
1 red pepper
1 yellow pepper
400 g red onion
350 g sausages
4 tbsp olive oil
salt and black pepper
50 g plain flour
1 egg
100 ml milk
4 tbsp Greek yoghurt
1 tbsp creamed horseradish or to taste

1.   Preheat the oven to 220/fan 200/gas 7.
2.   Cut the vegetables into equally sized large chunks. Place in a bowl, coat in olive oil and season. Arrange on a large baking tray lined with baking parchment, with the sausages tucked among the vegetables. Roast for 25 minutes, turn the vegetables and return to the oven for a further 35 minutes.
3.   Make the Yorkshires 20 minutes before the vegetables are ready. Sift the flour into a bowl and season well. Whisk in the egg and milk until you have a smooth batter.

4.   Put ½ tsp oil in the base of a 12-hole mini muffin tin and place in the oven for five minutes to heat. Pour in the batter and bake for 15 minutes until golden.

5.   Meanwhile, mix the yoghurt and horseradish. Serve with the roasted vegetables, sausages and mini-Yorkshires.

Braised Red Cabbage with Lentils and Chorizo Sausage

I only discovered this recipe in recent years and we often have it for a Sunday night supper with baked potatoes and Greek yoghurt. A vegan version can be made without the sausage. I tend to pick out the sausage so that you have the spicy taste but that would not suit a committed vegetarian!

Serves 6

1 onion
1 kg red cabbage
1 medium cooking apple
60 ml white wine vinegar
120 ml apple juice
1 cinnamon stick
grating of nutmeg
1 tbsp brown sugar
200 g Puy lentils
240 g chorizo sausage
15 g parsley
salt and black pepper

1.   Preheat the oven to 160/140 fan/gas 3
2.   Slice the onion, red cabbage and apple using a food processor or by hand. Place in a large heatproof casserole. Sprinkle over the sugar and the nutmeg. Add the vinegar, apple juice and cinnamon stick. Season well and bake in the oven for two hours, or until tender, stirring halfway through.
3.   Meanwhile, put the lentils in a pan with just enough water to cover. Season with salt then simmer for 20 minutes until tender. Drain and set aside.

4.   Chop the chorizo into bite-sized pieces and fry until beginning to colour. (You won't need any fat as the chorizo will release fat while cooking.)
5.   To serve, remove the cabbage from the oven, stir through the lentils and sausage.
6.   Place the lentils in a pan with seasoned water to just cover them and simmer for 20 minutes until tender. Drain and set aside.
7.   Chop the parsley. Remove the cabbage from the oven stir through the lentils and sausage, sprinkle with parsley and serve.

Cheesy Pasta Bake

Once you have the ragu sauce this is a fairly easy supper to make. You could even make it with leftover chilli con carne.

Serves 4

Half quantity of ragu (see page 65)
300 g penne pasta
50 g butter
30 g flour
500 ml milk
100 g cheddar cheese
25 g parmesan
salt and black pepper

1.   Preheat the oven fan 180/200/gas 6
2.   Cook the penne pasta according to the pack instructions in a large pan of boiling water. Drain and set aside.
3.   Make the cheese sauce. Melt the butter, add the flour and cook by stirring over a medium-low heat for one minute. Add the milk gradually, stirring all the time. Once all the milk is added, cook for five minutes, stirring all the time; the finished sauce should be the consistency of pouring cream. Grate the cheddar and stir into the sauce. Season, then add the pasta.
4.   Place half the pasta mixture in a large ovenproof dish and cover with the ragu. Finish with the rest of the pasta mixture layered on top.
5.   Grate the parmesan and sprinkle over the pasta. Bake for 35 minutes until golden.
6.   Serve with lots of green vegetables or a crisp green salad.

Goat's Cheese Soufflé

I have been making this for over 15 years and it is very simple and a bit more good-natured than a traditional soufflé. It can be served as a starter or as a main course; it is quite rich so I like lots of green vegetables on the side.

Serves 6 as a starter or 4 as a main course

25 g butter

200 g parmesan

400 g soft goat's cheese (without rind)

6 eggs, separated

150 ml double cream

1 tsp fresh chopped thyme

1.   Preheat the oven to 200/180/gas 6

2.   Melt the butter and grease six gratin dishes or ovenproof soup plates. Grate the parmesan and sprinkle two tbsp into the dishes.

3.   Place the apostrophe goat's cheese into a large bowl and whisk until smooth. Add the egg yolks and whisk again until smooth. Stir in the cream, thyme, seasoning and half the remaining parmesan.

4.   In a clean dry bowl, whisk the egg whites until stiff. Stir one tbsp of the egg whites briskly into the goat's cheese mixture, then carefully fold in the remaining egg white to retain as much air as possible. Sprinkle with remaining parmesan.

5.   Divide equally among the dishes and place in the oven for 12 minutes until risen and golden. Serve immediately.

Pan Haggerty

Although my maternal grandfather was from Yorkshire, I do not remember this traditional Yorkshire recipe being served in his house. I do remember he had to have large Yorkshire puddings served with gravy before the main roast dinner was served. I have been cooking pan haggerty since the mid-1980s. It is vegetarian and economical to make, however, in the interest of keeping the meat eaters happy, I would usually serve it with bacon. A food processor with the slicing attachment makes very quick work of slicing the onions and potatoes.

Serves 4

450 g potatoes
250 g onions
2 tbsp olive oil
salt and black pepper
100 g grated cheddar cheese

1.   Thinly slice the potatoes and onions.
2.   Heat the oil in a large frying pan. Layer up the potatoes and onions in the pan, seasoning as you go. Finally, top with the grated cheese.
3.   Cover the pan with a lid and fry on a very gentle heat for 30 minutes.
4.   Remove the lid and brown under a preheated grill. Serve from the pan.

A real comfort food if served with peas and tomato sauce

Pasta with Asparagus, Pea and Mint Pesto

I first made this over 20 years ago and still look forward to it when it is the asparagus season. The pesto is more like a creamy sauce than a traditional pesto. If you are not vegetarian, it is delicious topped with a few slices of fried prosciutto.

Serves 2

170 g frozen peas
2 tbsp fresh mint, roughly chopped
3 tbsp olive oil
110 g crème fraîche
170 g spaghetti
250 g fresh asparagus trimmed and cut into 5 cm lengths
salt and black pepper
grated parmesan to serve

1.   Cook the peas in boiling water for five minutes, add the mint and strain, reserving the cooking liquid.
2.   Put the peas and mint in a food processor with three tbsp oil, crème fraiche and seasoning. Set to one side.
3.   In a large saucepan of boiling water cook the spaghetti according to the pack instructions, adding the asparagus three minutes before the end of the cooking time. Drain and return to the pan. Stir in the pea sauce and six tbsp of the reserved liquid and warm over a low heat. Serve at once sprinkled with grated parmesan.

Pasta with Tomatoes and Rocket

After 25 years, I never tire of this light and simple but very tasty supper dish. It is one of the first things I cooked for Marc, so I had to include it in this book.

Serves 4

400 g dried orecchiette pasta or any shape of your choice
Olive oil
2 tbsp pine nuts
450 g cherry tomatoes, halved (a combination of red and yellow works well)
90 g rocket
Salt and black pepper
Parmesan shavings to serve

1.   In a large saucepan of boiling water cook the spaghetti according to the pack instructions.
2.   Meanwhile, add one tbsp of oil to a pan and cook the pine nuts for one minute until golden. Add the tomatoes and cook for one minute until heated through.
3.   Drain the pasta. Return to the saucepan with two tbsp of oil and the rocket to heat through. Add the tomatoes and pine nuts, stir carefully to mix together then serve scattered with parmesan shavings.

Potato and Mushroom Risotto

This sound a very unlikely recipe and you do have to keep an eye on it, but the result is worth it. It has become a popular Friday night supper and is rather nice with a glass of white wine.

Serves 4

80 g onions, finely chopped
butter
800 g potatoes (Maris piper or King Edwards), peeled and cut into 1 cm squares
30 ml white wine
600 ml hot vegetable stock
450 g chestnut mushrooms, washed and sliced
100 ml double cream
15 g parsley, chopped
salt and black pepper
grated parmesan to serve

1. Using a large pan sweat the onions in a knob butter without browning. After five minutes, add the potatoes and continue to cook for a further five minutes.
2. Add the wine and cook until evaporated. Reduce the heat to low and slowly add the vegetable stock a little at a time.
3. Continue adding the liquid until the potatoes are tender; you may need more or less liquid than stated depending on the potatoes you use. Season.
4. In a separate pan, fry the sliced mushrooms in a knob of butter until they are browned. Add the cream, half the parsley and seasoning and warm through.
5. Divide the potato risotto among four warmed bowls, top with mushrooms and remaining parsley. Serve with grated parmesan.

Ragu

A ragu is a great slow-cooked meat dish that can be served with pasta such as fettuccine or as the filling in lasagne or a pasta bake. It is a superior version of a Bolognese sauce and the slow cooking gives a wonderful flavour. It freezes well so make a batch for quick pasta suppers.

Serves 8–10

Olive oil
1 large onion, chopped
150 g cubed pancetta
500 g minced beef
500 g minced pork
2 x 400 g tins chopped tomatoes
70 g tomato purée
150 ml red wine
150 ml beef or vegetable stock
¼ grated nutmeg
15 g fresh basil
Salt and black pepper

1.   Preheat the oven to 120 fan/140/gas 1
2.   Set a saucepan with one tbsp olive oil over a medium-low heat. Cook the onion until it has softened but not browned. Add the pancetta and cook for a further five minutes. Transfer to a large ovenproof casserole.

3.   Add one tbsp of oil to the pan. Set over a very high heat then brown the beef before transferring to the casserole. Repeat with the pork.

4.   Add the tomatoes, purée, stock and nutmeg to the casserole and stir to combine. Chop the basil, add to the casserole, season generously and bring to a simmer.

5.   Place in the oven without a lid and cook for four hours. Check and stir a couple of times before the end of the cooking time; the sauce should be reduced and thick with very little liquid left.

6.   Serve with tagliatelle or pasta of your choice and grated parmesan cheese.

Use for the base of lasagne or cheesy pasta bake

Red Lentil Pasta Sauce

I bought my first vegetarian cookbook in 1986 and found a recipe for red lentil sauce. It has evolved since I first started making it, but it is my Bolognese substitute. The first Bolognese sauce we had when I was young was a tin of meat, a tin of Campbell's spaghetti sauce and a tin of tomatoes all mixed together. Not something I hanker after today.

Serves 4

Olive oil
1 onion, finely chopped
1 red pepper, quartered, deseeded and chopped
1 garlic clove
175 g red lentils
1 x 400 g can tomatoes
70 g tomato purée
2 tsp dried oregano
500 ml vegetable stock
1 tbsp lemon juice
Salt and black pepper
Grated parmesan to serve

1.   Heat one tbsp of olive oil in a large saucepan and sauté the onion, garlic and red pepper over a low heat for ten minutes or beginning to soften.
2.   Add the red lentils to the pan followed by the tomatoes, tomato purée, oregano and 450 ml of the stock. Stir and simmer gently for 30 minutes. Check from time to time adding more stock as needed. Season to taste.
3.   Serve with pasta of your choice and grated parmesan.

I love this the next day cold with pita bread – a bit like a lentil dip.

Spiced Tomatoes with Naan Bread

If you fancy a starter before a curry and do not have the time to make samosas, then this is a handy recipe. It also makes a tasty lunch.

Serves 2 for lunch or 4 as a starter

Butter
Olive oil
4 mini naan bread for starter or 2 large naans for lunch
2 garlic cloves, crushed
1 tsp ground coriander
1 tsp ground cumin
pinch of dried red chilli flakes
8 medium tomatoes, quartered or 400 g cherry tomatoes, halved
salt and black pepper
2 tbsp fresh coriander, chopped

1.   Brush the naan bread with butter and place under a just warm grill.
2.   Heat some olive oil in a pan and fry the garlic and spices until sizzling. Add the tomatoes and cook for about four minutes until they begin to soften. Season.
3.   Increase the heat of the grill and lightly toast naan bread. Serve the naan with the tomatoes piled on top and sprinkled with the chopped coriander.

Creamy Lamb Curry

Until the 1980s, the only curry I had made or tasted was made with curry powder, which does not reflect the subtlety of Indian cuisine. I have been making this recipe since the 1989, it is mild but very tasty. Vicki learned to make it when she was ill, it became one of the few things she ever used a recipe for.

Serves 4–6

Sunflower oil
1 kg leg of lamb cut into cubes
6 cloves
2.5 cm cinnamon stick
10 cardamom pods
200 g onions, peeled and finely chopped
2.5 cm fresh ginger, grated
2 garlic cloves, crushed
1 tsp ground coriander
2 tsp ground cumin
½ tsp cayenne pepper
50 g ground almonds
1 tsp salt
200 ml double cream
½ tsp garam masala

1.   Preheat the oven fan 160/180/gas 4.
2.   Set a large frying pan with two tbsp oil over a high heat. Brown the meat in batches until brown on all sides. Remove and transfer to a large ovenproof casserole.

3.   Add one tbsp oil to the frying pan and stir in the cloves, cinnamon and cardamom. Add the onions and cook until golden brown. Add the ginger, garlic, ground spices, six tbsp water and the ground almonds. Stir and cook for three minutes until begins to turn brown. Transfer to the casserole dish.
4.   Add salt, cream and 200 ml water. Bring to the boil, cover and transfer to the oven. Cook for approximately 1½ hours, stirring occasionally.
5.   Sprinkle with garam masala and serve, reminding your guests about the whole spices they may find. Serve with plain rice and cucumber raita.

This curry improves in flavour if cooked the day before and reheated in the oven for 30 minutes.

Khichri

Kedgeree was a regular meal I made in the 1980s; this is the Indian recipe that the British adapted into kedgeree, it is a very simple dish of lentils and rice. I have been cooking this since 1988 when I served it for supper to a vegetarian friend. I serve it as a meal on its own with cucumber raita, but you can serve it as a side to a curry.

Serves 4

225 g red lentils
225 g white basmati rice
100 g butter
2 medium onions, peeled and thinly sliced
2 garlic cloves, peeled and crushed
1 tsp ground cumin
2 bay leaves
1 x 8 cm cinnamon stick
4 cloves
4 cardamom pods, crushed
850 ml water
salt and black pepper
15 g fresh coriander, chopped

1.   Wash the lentils and place in a bowl and cover with cold water. Do the same with the rice in a separate bowl.

2.   Melt the butter in a large pan. Add the sliced onions and fry over a very gentle heat for about ten minutes until golden brown, adding the garlic halfway through the cooking time. Transfer the onions to a plate, keeping some of the melted butter in the pan.

3.   Drain the rice and the lentils then add to the pan and toss in the remaining fat. Stir in the ground cumin then add the water. Add the remaining spices, one tsp of salt and plenty of black pepper. Stir once, lower the heat, cover and simmer very gently for 15 minutes, or until the rice and lentils are tender and most of the liquid has been absorbed. If the rice and lentils are not cooked, you may need to add a little more water; the finished dish should be moist rather than dry.

4.   Add the reserved onions, half the coriander then check the seasoning. Serve sprinkled with the remaining coriander.

Cucumber Raita

Serves 4

1 cucumber
300 ml natural yoghurt (I prefer Greek as it gives a creamier result)
½ tsp ground cumin
Salt and black pepper

1.   Coarsely grate the cucumber into a bowl. Extract and discard as much liquid as possible by squeezing the cucumber.
2.   Mix in the yoghurt and cumin, seasoning to taste.
3.   Cover and chill until ready to serve.

Any leftovers can be eaten with toasted pita bread for a quick lunch.

Red Lentil and Sweet Potato Dhal

This is a recipe that combines dhal, sag aloo and a veggie curry in a great one-pot dish. It tastes just as good the next day although the lentils will become softer on reheating. A great Friday night curry supper.

Serves 6

1 tbsp olive oil
1 medium onion, chopped
1 tbsp finely chopped ginger
1 tsp ground coriander
1 tsp ground cumin
1 tsp dried chilli flakes
1 tsp garam masala
4 cardamom pods
250 g red lentils
1 x 400 g chopped tomatoes
400 ml low-fat coconut milk
600 g sweet potato, peeled and chopped into 2 cm pieces
200 g spinach
2 tbsp lemon juice
Salt

1.   Set a large saucepan with the olive oil over a low heat. Cook the onions for five minutes. Add the ginger, cook for two minutes, then stir in the spices and cook for one more minute.

2.   Add the lentils, tomatoes, coconut milk and 400 ml water. Bring to the boil, stir in the sweet potato and gently simmer for 30 minutes, stirring every ten minutes until the sweet potato is tender; you may need to add more water.

3.   Season to taste then add the spinach. Leave for a couple of minutes until wilted. Finish the dhal with lemon juice.

Serve with rice or naan bread.

Creamy Smoked Haddock Chowder

The children used to love this chowder and when I lived in Hexham in the late 1980s there was a great fish shop. It makes a hearty lunch or a simple supper. Serve it with crusty bread.

Serves 6

450 g fresh haddock fillet (or any firm white fish)
225 g smoked haddock fillet
butter
350 g onion, thinly sliced
175 g courgettes, chopped into 1 cm thick slices
175 g carrots, peeled and chopped into 1 cm thick slices
350 g potatoes, peeled and cut into 2 cm chunks
600 ml vegetable stock
125 g cooked peeled prawns
1 level tbsp cornflour
150 ml single cream
15 g chopped fresh parsley
Salt and black pepper

1.   Skin the fish and cut into large chunks.
2.   Melt a knob of butter in a large heatproof casserole or large saucepan. Add the onions, courgettes and carrots and sauté gently for four minutes.
3.   Add the stock and the potatoes then cover and simmer gently for 30 minutes until all the vegetables are tender.
4.   Add the fish and the prawns and return to the heat for a further five minutes until the fish is cooked.
5.   Mix the cornflour to a smooth paste with a little water carefully stir into the casserole and cook for one minute stirring all the time. Just before serving stir in the cream, parsley and seasoning.

Warm Squash and Lentil Salad with Halloumi

We are lucky enough to grow squash and onions in the garden, so this uses up produce that last throughout the winter. Halloumi has been around for thousands of years, but I only discovered it in 2001 and it is now always in the fridge.

Serves 2

250 g butternut squash, peeled, deseeded and chopped into bite-sized chunks
1 red onion, cut into 8 wedges
olive oil
1tsp ground cumin
salt and black pepper
250 g pack ready-to-eat Puy lentils
1 tbsp red wine vinegar
70 g baby leaf spinach
250 g halloumi, sliced

1.   Preheat the oven to 200 fan/220/gas 7. Put the squash and onion in a roasting tin and toss with 1 tbsp olive oil and the cumin. Season then roast on a baking tray lined with baking parchment for 20 minutes, or until tinged brown and the squash is soft.
2.   Heat the lentils in a microwave according to the instructions. Tip into a large bowl with the vinegar, two tbsp oil, spinach and vegetables. Divide between warm bowls or plates.
3.   Heat ½ tbsp oil in a frying pan over a medium-high heat. Fry the halloumi for a few minutes on each side until golden brown. Top the salad with the halloumi and serve immediately.

Winter Squash Gratin

Marc describes this as one of his favourites, he does have quite a few favourites and I would not be able to include them all. This produces a creamy sauce so serve it with a baked potato, you will not need any additional butter. You could make it at any time of the year, but it is rich and comforting, ideal for a winter's evening.

Serves 4 as a side dish or 2 as a main

1 kg squash, peeled, deseeded and cut into 3 cm chunks
2 tsp fresh thyme
olive oil
400 g large tomatoes
60 g goat's cheese with rind
140 ml double cream
75 g Gruyère or cheddar cheese, grated
salt and black pepper

1.   Preheat the oven 180 fan/200/gas 6. Toss the squash in a roasting with one tbsp olive oil, the thyme and seasoning. Roast for 20–25 minutes until squash is browning at the edges.
2.   Peel the tomatoes by placing in boiling water for one minute then slip off the skins. Cut into chunks.
3.   Place the squash and tomatoes in an ovenproof, shallow serving dish. Cube the goat's cheese and dot around dish. Pour over cream, sprinkle with grated cheese and bake for 20 minutes until golden.

Squash and Green Bean Tagine

This is a great vegan main course, served with couscous. I have been making this for over ten years. It tastes just as good reheated the next day, although the beans will not be as green. It can be served as a side dish if preferred.

Serves 4

Olive oil
1 large onion, finely chopped
1tsp ground cumin
1 tsp ground cinnamon
2 tsp harissa paste (or to taste)
4 plum tomatoes, peeled and chopped
500 g butternut squash, peeled and cut into 2 cm cubes
250 g green beans, trimmed and cut into 3 cm pieces
20 pitted black olives
juice of ½lemon
15 g chopped coriander (optional)
salt and black pepper

1.   Heat the oil in a large heatproof casserole. Cook the onion over a medium-low heat for ten minutes until softened but not browned. Add the spices and harissa and cook for one minute.
2.   Add the tomatoes, followed by the squash and green beans. Add 200 ml water, cover and simmer for 35–40 minutes until the squash is soft. Season then stir in the lemon juice, coriander (if using) and black olives. Serve the tagine with couscous.

Taleggio Risotto with Walnut Pesto

I have been making a four-cheese risotto since the late 1980s when soft Italian cheese was much harder to come by. Nowadays there is a much wider variety of cheese available and this is a lighter version.

Serves 4

Pesto
50 g walnuts, toasted in a medium oven for 7 minutes
25 g flat leaf parsley, roughly chopped
75 ml olive oil
25 g grated parmesan

Risotto
20 g butter
2 leeks, washed, halved and thinly sliced
300 g risotto rice
1tsp chopped fresh thyme
100 ml dry white wine or 4 tbsp dry vermouth
750 ml hot vegetable stock
200 g taleggio cheese
salt and black pepper

1. Place all the pesto ingredients in a food processor and whizz until smooth. Season to taste and set aside.
2. For the risotto, heat the butter in a large pan and sauté leeks until they are soft but not brown. Add the rice and thyme to the pan and stir over the heat for a couple of minutes.
3. Pour in the wine and allow to evaporate over the heat.
4. Add the stock about 70 ml at a time, stirring constantly. Continue until the rice is almost cooked but the grains still have a bite to them (al dente). Use as much stock as you need; you may need more or less than given above.
5. Cut the taleggio into bite-sized chunks and add to the risotto, stir and leave for a couple of minutes for the cheese to soften, then season to taste. Serve in individual bowls with a spoonful of pesto on top.

Pea Tart

I first made this in 2006 and it is probably Marc's absolute favourite supper. You can use ready-made short crust pastry but homemade has a better flavour. You could make some pastry for the freezer so that you have it ready to hand. This tart is a beautiful colour with a delicate flavour. A rocket salad is the perfect accompaniment.

Serves 6

Pastry
100 g chilled butter, cubed
200 g plain flour
1 egg yolk
about 40 ml cold water

Filling
250 g leeks, thinly sliced
2 tbsp olive oil
250 g frozen peas, defrosted
300 ml double cream
3 eggs
½tsp caster sugar
½tsp salt
1 tbsp lemon juice
salt and black pepper

1.   Use a food processor to make the pastry or do this by hand. Rub the butter into the flour until it resembles fine breadcrumbs then add the water and egg yolk to combine into a ball that leaves the sides of the bowl. Chill for 20 minutes.
2.   Preheat the oven to 180 fan/200/gas 6.
3.   Roll out the pastry and line a 23 cm flan tin. Ensure that the pastry is

pushed into the edges of the tin and trim. Chill for 20 minutes.

4.   For the filling, cook the leeks in the oil over a low heat for 10 minutes. You want to soften but not brown them.

5.   Place the peas in a food processor and blitz for a few seconds. Add the rest of the ingredients and blitz again briefly until combined. Season well.

6.   Place the leeks in the base of the tart and carefully pour over the pea mixture. Bake for a further 30 minutes until golden and just set.

Tomato and Parmesan Tart

A tasty tomato tart that I have been making for over 20 years. A great way to use up a glut of tomatoes and the parmesan crust makes a great alternative to pastry. Makes for a lovely summer supper.

Serves 4–6

75 g plain flour
75 g butter
140 g finely grated parmesan
¼ tsp cayenne pepper
900 g tomatoes, plum work well
4 tbsp sun-dried tomato paste
15 g fresh breadcrumbs
1 heaped tsp chopped fresh thyme
Salt and black pepper

1.   Place the flour, butter, 75 g parmesan, cayenne pepper and ½tsp salt in a food processor. Blend until looks like rough breadcrumbs. (You can do this by hand, but this method is much quicker). Set aside ⅓of the crumb mixture.
2.   Line a 24 cm square tin with parchment and press the remaining crumb mixture into the base. Chill for ten minutes. Preheat the oven to fan 160/180/gas
3.   Bake the tart base for about 15 minutes until golden brown. Leave to cool.
4.   Cut the tomatoes into halves or thirds depending on their size. Spread the tomato paste over the tart base and sprinkle with half the breadcrumbs. Place the tomato slices over the base and scatter with thyme. Top with the remaining breadcrumbs, parmesan and pastry crumb mixture. Season.
5.   Bake the tart for a further 15–20 minutes until golden brown. Cool slightly.
6.   Serve warm or at room temperature.

Feta Tarts

I first ate feta when I went to a Greek Island in 1978 when it was served as part of a Greek salad, but I did not start using this tasty cheese a great deal until I discovered this recipe in the 1990s. If you keep a packet of pastry in the freezer this is pretty much a store-cupboard supper as all the ingredients have a long shelf life.

Serves 4

320 g ready-rolled puff pastry
2 tbsp olive oil
700 g red onions, thinly sliced
100 g sun dried tomatoes, chopped
80 g capers
25 g pine nuts
200 g feta, cubed
salt and black pepper

1.   Preheat the oven to 200/220 fan/gas 7. Place a large baking sheet in the oven.
2.   Unroll the pastry and cut into four equal size pieces. Place on a sheet of baking parchment. Score a border around each square 2 cm from the edge. Transfer to the baking sheet and bake for 10–15 minutes, until golden and puffed up. Remove from the oven and use a fork to push down the middle.
3.   Heat one tbsp oil in a pan and cook the onions over a low heat, stirring occasionally until the onions are soft and caramelised; this will take about ten minutes.
4.   Spread equal amounts of onion in the middle of each tart. Top with sun-dried tomatoes, capers, feta and pine nuts. Season and drizzle with the remaining oil.
5.   Bake for 15 minutes or until the pastry is golden. Serve.

Serve with a green salad and a tomato salad.

Goat's Cheese Parcels

I first started using goat's cheese in 1986 and since then it is regularly included in my weekly menus. This is a particularly rich and warming supper. I use basil pesto for this recipe but any flavour of pesto works well. I keep a mini tape measure in the kitchen to ensure that where a recipe requires a certain size of tin or dimension of pastry, I can double check it.

Serves 4

500 g block of puff pastry
4 individual goat's cheese, approx. 70 g each
4 dessertspoons of pesto
1 egg, beaten
15 g grated parmesan

1.   Preheat the oven 200/180 fan/gas 6
2.   Roll out the pastry to 40 x 36 cm and then cut into 4 equal sized rectangles.
3.   Place one spoonful of pesto in the centre of each piece of pastry and top with the individual goat's cheese.
4.   Brush the edges of the pastry with the egg, fold over the filling and seal securely down the centre and at both ends, trimming any excess pastry. Turn the parcels over and place on a baking sheet lined with parchment.
5.   Brush with egg and sprinkle with parmesan cheese.
6.   Bake in the oven for 20 minutes until the pastry is golden brown.

Serve with a baked potato to help mop up all the melted goat's cheese and seasonal green vegetables.

5. My Life in the Kitchen
1990–2000

For me, the 1990s were influenced by Delia Smith's straight forward recipes and she introduced me to new ingredients and ideas for entertaining family and friends. I also admired Raymond Blanc but not all his recipes were conducive to being a relaxed host whilst serving great dinner party food.

During this time, I experimented with ice-cream makers and pasta makers but the highlight of this era was my salad spinner. A great 1970s invention that has made washing and drying salad and leaf vegetables so much easier than the tea towel shake.

It was around this time I also discovered carrot cake, a wonderful combination of cake and creamy topping, possibly my favourite cake to this day. A wider variety of food was becoming available and travelling broadened the mind as well as my own culinary outlook. I had never heard of granola until a visit to the States.

The introduction of skimmed milk was a relief to me, having been forced to drink warm creamy milk at school.

As a family we settled in Kent in a lovely house with a slightly tired farmhouse kitchen. Regardless of the state of the kitchen we still managed to have regular dinner parties as well as producing family meals. I was working part-time so I became adept at producing nutritious meals in super quick time.

Online shopping had just become available in the late 1990s, but I used to do a big shop in my lunch hour so by planning ahead I had an exact list of what I needed and was able to whizz around.

I was still cooking a roast lunch every Sunday but on the whole, we were eating far less meat and I was increasingly able to sneak in the odd vegetarian meal without anyone really noticing.

Juggling work and family life became incredibly challenging when Martin was first diagnosed with one cancer and then a year later, another. His terminal diagnosis made life very hard, but we still had to eat. In May 1998, we organised a huge party, billed as a Cole celebration. Catering for 135 people kept me occupied and all our family and friends thought everything must be OK. At the time only we knew of the terrible prognosis. We also spent time planning a lovely new kitchen which sadly was not fitted before Martin died aged just 44 in December 1998.

Example weekly menus from 1990's

Sunday
Fast roast pork with rosemary and apples with roasted vegetables
Fromage fraise creams

Monday
Smoked haddock risotto
Fruit salad

Tuesday
Chicken with gingered noodles (recipe page 50)

Wednesday
Salmon pie with green beans
Pineapple

Thursday
Goat's cheese soufflé (recipe page 58)

Friday
Tarts spaghetti (recipe page 44)

Saturday, 16 May 1998
A Cole celebration
Chicken liver and pistachio pate with melba toast and French bread
Chicken with lime and ginger mayonnaise
Roast ham
Poached salmon
Green salad, tomato and basil salad, mixed pepper salad, bean salad, new potatoes
Raspberry shortbread stacks (recipe page 152)

Feeding Friends / Entertaining

Marinated Cheese and Chilli Salad

This a great recipe for a crowd as it can prepared the day before and is so tasty. There are so many people I have served this to over the years and I have shared the recipe time and again. It is a bit more interesting than the 1990s favourite of grilled goat's cheese. I like to serve it with roasted red peppers or roasted beef tomatoes. I promised Izzy and Tracey that this would be included in my book, it has taken me sometime but here it is.

Serves 4-6

250 g ricotta cheese
300 g soft goat's cheese
75 g finely grated parmesan cheese
2 egg whites
salt and black pepper
150 ml olive oil
1 level tsp Dijon mustard
2 tsp balsamic vinegar
pinch caster sugar
½ green chilli
1 tbsp capers

1.   Preheat the oven to 180 fan/200/ gas 6.
2.   Using a hand mixer, mix together the ricotta, goat's cheese, parmesan and egg whites. Season.
3.   Line a 24 cm square baking tin with parchment. Spoon in the cheese mixture and carefully drizzle over 25 ml of the oil. Bake for 20 minutes until set. Cool.
4.   Mix together the mustard, vinegar and caster sugar to form a paste and slowly whisk in the remaining olive oil. Deseed the chilli, thinly slice, stir into the dressing with the capers and set aside.
5.   Remove the cheese from the tin, using the baking parchment to help you. Cut the cheese into 16 squares and carefully layer in a large ovenproof dish. Spoon over the dressing cover and marinade overnight.
6.   Before serving, warm the cheese in the oven 160 fan/180/gas 5 for five minutes.

Serve on its own with plenty of bread or with roasted red peppers or tomatoes.

Roasted Red Peppers

I first made stuffed peppers at school in the 1970s; they were green and filled with mince. Red peppers are so much sweeter and tastier, and they do not need anything other than the simplest of fillings. These can be served as a starter on their own with a few rocket leaves.

1 red pepper per person
1 medium tomato per person
Olive oil
Seasoning
Basil leaves to serve

1.   Preheat the oven to 160/180/gas 5
2.   Cut the peppers in half, retain the stalk intact but remove the seeds and any white parts.
3.   Skin the tomatoes by placing in boiling water for one minute and then removing the skin. Cut the tomatoes into quarters and place two quarters in each pepper half.
4.   Place the pepper halves in a large roasting tin. Drizzle one tbsp of olive oil over two pepper halves and season with salt and pepper.
5.   Roast for 50 minutes to one hour until the edges begin to char.
6.   Remove from the oven and transfer to a serving platter to cool. Scatter torn basil leaves on top.

Roasted Tomatoes

1 large beef tomato per person
garlic
olive oil
salt and black pepper
fresh basil

1.   Preheat the oven to 180/200/gas 6
2.   Halve the tomatoes, place in a roasting tin cut side uppermost. Drizzle over one tsp of oil over each half, a small amount of chopped garlic and seasoning.
3.   Roast for 45 minutes to an hour, until the edges begin to char.
4.   Remove from the oven and transfer to a serving platter to cool. Scatter torn basil leaves on top before serving.

Baked Mushrooms with Sourdough Toast

This recipe was billed in the 1980s as a demonstration of how delicious vegetarian food could be. It makes a great starter but could even be served as a light lunch.

Serves 6 as a starter

500 g chestnut mushrooms or a mixture of mushrooms if you prefer
75 g butter
25 g coriander, chopped
1 tsp ground coriander
30 ml lemon juice
30 ml olive oil
6 thick slices of sourdough bread
1 garlic clove
100 ml single cream (optional)
salt and black pepper

1.   Preheat the oven to 180/200/gas 6.
2.   Thinly slice the mushrooms and place in an ovenproof dish dotted with half the butter. Sprinkle over 1 tbsp of the chopped coriander and the ground coriander, lemon juice, olive oil and seasoning.
3.   Cover the dish with foil and bake for 35 minutes. Stir halfway through the cooking time.
4.   Rub the slices of sourdough with the garlic and spread with the remaining butter. Place in the oven with the mushrooms for the final ten minutes of cooking time.
5.   Remove the bread and mushrooms from the oven. Stir the cream, if using, into the mushrooms.
6.   Plate up the bread slices and top with mushrooms and remaining chopped coriander.

Twice Baked Cauliflower Cheese Soufflés

It was the late 1990s when I first discovered the joy of twice baked soufflés. They are prepared in advance and make a stunning starter. There are lots of different variations of the soufflé but this is my favourite, light with a delicate flavour. Plate up the side salad slightly before the soufflés are ready so you can serve immediately.

Serves 8

50 g butter, plus extra for greasing
25 g ground almonds
250 g cauliflower florets
150 ml milk
40 g plain flour
75 g cheddar cheese, finely grated
75 g Emmental cheese, finely grated
3 eggs, separated
salt and black pepper
300 ml double cream
1 level tbsp grain mustard

1. Preheat the oven 180/ fan 160/ gas 4. Base line with baking parchment 8 dariole molds or ramekins and grease well with a little melted butter.
2. Cook the almonds under a preheated grill turning until lightly toasted. Dust the moulds with the ground almonds.
3. Cook the cauliflower for 5–10 minutes until just tender, drain and plunge into cold water before draining again. Place in a food processor with the milk and process until smooth.
4. Melt the 50 g butter in a pan then add the flour, stirring to make a smooth paste. Beat in the cauliflower purée and bring to the boil. Cool a little before stirring in the cheese and egg yolks. Season well. Whisk the egg whites to soft peaks and carefully fold into the cauliflower mixture.

5.   Fill the moulds with the mixture and place in a roasting tin. Add enough hot water to come halfway up the moulds and bake for 20–25 minutes until firm to touch.

6.   Remove from the roasting tin and cool completely. Run a knife around the edge of the moulds and carefully turn out the soufflés onto a baking sheet.

7.   Pour the cream into a saucepan and bring to the boil and bubble until reduced by one third. Stir in the mustard and season. The soufflés and the sauce can be stored separately overnight in the fridge at this point.

8.   When ready to serve spoon a little of the sauce over the soufflés and bake in an oven 200/fan 180/gas 6 for 15 minutes until golden. Serve immediately.

Serve with a few halved cherry tomatoes and rocket, drizzled with a little olive oil and thick balsamic vinegar.

Mushroom Samosas

These are very tasty little bites ideal as a starter. If you are having a curry supper for friends or family, they are well worth the effort. You will need a tape measure and once you have folded a couple it becomes really easy. You can make them in advance and cook them in the oven just before you want to eat them.

Makes approx. 20

2.5 cm root ginger, finely chopped
2 garlic cloves, crushed
2 tbsp full fat natural yoghurt
25 g butter
125 g onion, finely chopped
1 tsp cumin seeds
pinch of cayenne pepper
225 g chestnut mushrooms, finely chopped
125 g potato, finely diced
salt and black pepper
125 g frozen peas
2 tbsp chopped coriander
300 g filo pastry
vegetable oil for brushing

1.   Combine the ginger, garlic and yoghurt. Set aside.
2.   Heat the butter in a pan over a medium-low heat. Cook the onion until soft then stir in the spices and cook for 30 seconds more. Add the chopped mushrooms, increase the heat and cook for a few minutes until all the moisture is evaporated.
3.   Add the yoghurt mixture, potatoes and 150 ml water, bring to the boil, cover and simmer gently for 25 minutes or until the potatoes are cooked and nearly all the liquid has been absorbed. Add the peas five minutes before the end of the cooking time. Stir in the coriander and set aside to cool.

4.   Cut the filo into 30 x 13 cm rectangles. Brush lightly with oil, fold in half to give 30 x 6.5 cm strips. Brush lightly with oil again and place about two tsp of the samosas filling in the bottom left had corner. Fold the filo over to form a rectangle and continue to fold until the filling is enclosed in several layers and you have a neat triangular parcel. Repeat with the rest of the filo and filling. Place samosas on a baking tray and give one final brush with oil. They can be stored in the fridge for a few hours until you are ready to cook them.

5.   When you are ready to serve preheat the oven to 200/fan 180/ gas 6. Cook the samosas for 10–15 minutes until deep golden brown.

Serve with cucumber raita and mango or chilli chutney.

Duck Confit

I have been making duck confit for over 25 years now and it is a brilliant dish for a crowd. It can be made several weeks in advance and stored covered in the fat until needed. Although I find a lot of meat difficult to digest, this duck is cooked slowly for so long that the meat almost melts when you eat it. Although it uses lots of fat in the initial cooking this is all discarded so the end result is rich, flavoursome with a crispy skin but not at all fatty.

2 bay leaves
few sprigs fresh thyme
4 garlic cloves, peeled and crushed
40 g sea salt
black pepper
4 duck legs
2 tablespoons olive oil
500 g duck or goose fat
200 g lard

1.	Break up the bay leaves and combine with the thyme, garlic, sea salt and plenty of black pepper. Rub the duck legs with the mixture, place in a bowl or dish cover and leave for in the fridge for 24 hours.
2.	Preheat the oven 140/fan 120/gas 1.
3.	Scrape off all the seasoning from the duck legs and reserve. Heat the oil in a frying pan and fry the duck legs skin-side down until golden brown.
4.	Put the duck legs skin side up in an ovenproof dish so they fit snugly. Scatter over the seasoning. Melt the duck or goose fat together with the lard and pour over to just about cover the duck. Place in the oven and cook for two hours. Remove from the oven and cool.

5.   When the duck has cooled, place the legs in a plastic storage box and pour the fat through a sieve until the legs are covered completely with the fat. Secure the box and place in the fridge until required.

6.   When you are ready to serve, preheat the oven to 230/fan 210/gas 8. Bring the duck legs to room temperature and scrape off as much fat as you can. (I wipe the legs with kitchen paper.)

7.   Place the legs skin-side down in a roasting tin and cook for five minutes. Drain off any melted fat, turn the legs over and cook for a further five minutes.

I serve this on a bed of mashed sweet potato with tender stem broccoli on the side in the winter and a bed of crushed peas with green beans and new potatoes on the side in the summer.

This recipe does not need a 'gravy' but if you want a sauce this does go very well.

Orange Sauternes Sauce

5 oranges
1 lemon
1 carrot
1 celery stalk
bouquet garni
1.5 litre vegetable stock
450 ml sweet white wine such as Sauternes
2 level tbsp caster sugar
2 tbsp fresh orange juice

1.   Cut the oranges, lemons, carrot and celery into pieces, place in a large saucepan with bouquet garni and stock. Bring to the boil and simmer uncovered for 45 minutes until reduced by half.
2.   Drain through a sieve, pressing through any juice. Discard the vegetables and fruit and return the sauce to the pan.
3.   Add the wine, sugar and orange juice. Bring to the boil and simmer for 45 minutes until syrupy.

Roasted Vegetable Strudel

I have been cooking this savoury strudel for 18 years and it makes for a great summer vegetarian supper party dish. You can also make it in advance and pop it in the oven to cook when you want to serve it. It is a bit more long-winded than some of the recipes in the book but worth the effort and meat eaters do not feel short-changed by having this served to them.

Serves 6

Roasted vegetables
2 medium courgettes
1 aubergine
450 g plum tomatoes
1 red pepper
1 yellow pepper
1 red onion
1 garlic clove
10 g basil leaves, torn
1 tsp coriander seeds, crushed
3 tbsp olive oil
salt and black pepper

Strudel
110 g pecan nuts
3 tbsp grated parmesan
75 g butter
1 x 270 g packet filo pastry sheets
110 g mozzarella, cubed

1.   Preheat the oven 220 fan/240/gas 9.
2.   Prepare the vegetables for the strudel. Cut the aubergine, courgette and onion into 2.5 cm dice. Deseed the peppers and cut into 2.5 cm squares. Finely chop the garlic. Peel the tomatoes by putting in boiling water for a couple of minutes and sliding off the skin, remove the seeds and cut into eight pieces.
3.   Place all the vegetables in a large roasting tin lined with baking parchment and scatter over the garlic, basil, coriander seeds and seasoning. Drizzle with oil and roast for 30 minutes until tender and beginning to brown at the edges. Remove from the oven and cool.
4.   To make the strudel lower the oven to 180/fan160/gas 4. Place the pecans on a baking tray and roast for six minutes. Once they are toasted remove from the oven and once cool pulse in a food processor until small. Mix with the parmesan.
5.   Melt the butter. Take a large sheet of baking parchment and lay 45 x 28 cm sheet of filo on top. (If your sheets are not this big then overlap a couple of sheets slightly using butter to secure the join). Brush the sheet of filo with butter and sprinkle over a quarter of the nut and parmesan mixture. Repeat this three times with the other filo sheets.
6.   Scatter half the mozzarella down the middle of the filo followed by the vegetables and the rest of the mozzarella. Leave a gap of five cm at each end.
7.   Using the parchment paper roll the filo over the filing lengthways and then over again so you have a seam under the strudel and tuck the edges underneath. Use the parchment to slide the strudel onto a baking tray. Brush with the rest of the butter and bake in the centre of the oven for 40 minutes until golden.

Salmon Fillets with Avocado Dressing

This recipe is a perfect summer lunch or supper party dish for however many people you are catering for. It can be served cold or warm and can be made in advance. I have been serving this to guests for over 25 years. The avocado dressing is popular with those who do not eat fish so if you are serving as part of a buffet make sure you make enough.

Serves 8

8 Salmon fillets approx. 120 g each
3 bay leaves
8 small sprigs of tarragon
8 tablespoons of white wine
Salt and Black pepper

Dressing
1 large ripe avocado or 2 small
300 ml creme fraiche
1 tsp balsamic vinegar
Salt and black pepper

1.   Pre heat the oven 180/160 fan/gas 4
2.   Take a large baking tray that will fit all the salmon fillets. Take a large sheet of foil, just over twice the size of the tray and place it centrally on the tray.
3.   Place each fillet on the tray and top each with a sprig of tarragon, piece of bay leaf, seasoning and white wine. Loosely bring together the foil and seal. Place in the oven for 15 minutes. Remove from the oven and cool while still encased in the foil. If serving straight away check the salmon is cooked through and return to the oven for a few minutes if necessary.
4.   For the dressing peel and chop the avocado reserving the stone. Place the avocado with the creme fraiche, balsamic and seasoning in a food processor and blend until smooth.
5.   Place in a serving bowl and if not serving straight away place the avocado stone in the middle to prevent too much discolouration. Remove stone and stir before serving.

Slow-Cooked Leg of Lamb

This is a very slow cooked leg of lamb and is in the oven for seven hours, although you can reduce that by following the timings below. I have always preferred to cook lamb in this way because it reduces the stress of roast timings. It is so easy to make and is very tasty. It makes for a great winter supper party or an Easter lunch. Even if you do not like anchovies you will not taste them in this, they will melt away and add a richness to the sauce. You do need to prep this the day before you want to cook it.

Serves 6–8

1 large leg of lamb (2 kg approx.)
1 tin of anchovies
olive oil
12 small onions
3 carrots
3 garlic cloves
2 bay leaves
3 sprigs of fresh thyme
75 ml brandy
1 bottle of wine red or white
vegetable stock
salt and black pepper

1.   The day before cooking, bone the leg of lamb and roll it securing with string (or get a butcher to do this for you). Push the anchovy fillets into the lamb where there are openings.
2.   On the day of cooking preheat the oven to 140 fan/160/gas 3.
3.   Heat the oil in a large casserole big enough for the leg of lamb. Brown the lamb on all sides then remove from the heat.

4.   Peel the onions (easier if you pop them in boiling water for a few minutes) cut into 3 cm chunks. Cut the carrots into 3 cm chunks and peel the garlic. Add the vegetables to the casserole with the bay leaves, thyme, brandy, wine, and seasoning. Add enough stock so that the liquid comes ⅔ up the meat.
5.   Bring to a simmer on the hob and cover. Place in the oven for seven hours.
6.   Remove the meat to a serving plate, remove the string and cut into chunks. Serve the vegetables and sauce separately.

This can be cooked in four hours at an oven temperature of 180/160 fan/gas 4. Serve with creamy dauphinoise potatoes or mash and seasonal green vegetables.

Lamb and Mint Meatball Tagine

The joy of sharing recipes is that you can introduce others to what can then become their own signature dish or family favourite. I made this for Rebecca and her husband Ant ten years ago and Ant has made it so many times since he does not need to read the recipe and it is their go-to supper party dish.

Serves 4

600 g minced lamb
1 garlic clove, crushed
1tsp ground coriander
2 tsp ground cumin
1 tsp hot paprika
3 tbsp chopped fresh mint
3 tbsp olive oil
2 medium onions, finely chopped
1 x 8 cm cinnamon stick
3 cm piece fresh ginger, finely grated
400 g chopped tomatoes
1 tbsp clear honey
150 ml lamb or chicken stock
1 tsp harissa paste
salt and black pepper

1.   To make the meatballs place the lamb, garlic, coriander, cumin, paprika, mint and seasoning in a large bowl and mix well. Shaped the mixture into about 20 x 2.5 cm balls.
2.   Heat two tbsp of the oil in a frying pan and fry the meatballs briefly on all sides. Transfer to a heatproof casserole.
3.   Heat the remaining one tbsp of oil in the frying pan. Gently cook the onions

for five minutes then add the cinnamon stick and ginger. Fry for a further two minutes until the onion is soft and beginning to colour. Add the tomatoes, honey, stock and harissa and bring to a simmer. Pour over the meatballs and return the casserole to the hob. Partly cover with a lid and simmer for a further 30 minutes, stirring occasionally. The sauce should be nicely thickened. Season and serve.

Serve with couscous or creamy mash.

Roasted Portabella Mushrooms

These mushrooms can be served on their own with creamy mash or topped with wilted spinach and taleggio. I have also served them as the vegetarian alternative to the chicken Supreme serving both on a bed of butter bean puree topped with romesco. I have given all options below so you can decide which is your favourite combination

Serves 4

8 large portabella or flat mushrooms
2 tsp fresh thyme leaves
8 tbsp olive oil
juice of 1 large lemon
Salt and black pepper

1.   Pre heat the oven to 180 fan/200/gas 6
2.   Wipe the mushrooms with a piece of damp kitchen towel. Place snugly in a large roasting tin.
3.   Mix the oil, lemon juice, thyme and seasoning and drizzle over the mushrooms.
4.   Cover the mushrooms with foil and bake for 25 minutes.

With Spinach and Taleggio

400 g washed spinach leaves wilted and coarsely chopped 250 g taleggio cut into 1 cm cubes.

Remove the mushrooms from the oven. Divide the spinach equally and top each mushroom, season. Finally place cubes of cheese on top of the spinach. Return to the oven uncovered for a further 8–10 minutes until the cheese is melted.

This goes well with the butter bean puree but I would not serve it with the romesco sauce as it will overwhelm the flavour of the spinach and cheese.

Romesco Sauce

This is a slightly spicy sauce that goes well with chicken as well as plain roasted mushrooms. It also can be eaten with pita bread as a tasty snack.

80 g stale white bread, torn
80 g blanched almonds, toasted in a pan
1½ tsp sherry vinegar
180 g roasted red peppers from a jar (such as Peppadew)
1 tsp sweet smoked paprika
½tsp hot paprika
1 garlic clove
120 ml olive oil
Squeeze of lemon juice

1.   Place all the ingredients apart from the oil and lemon juice in a food processor. With the motor running drizzle in the oil until a chunky paste is formed. Add seasoning and lemon juice to taste. Store for up to 24 hours in the fridge.

Bring to room temperature to serve.

Butter Bean Purée

Olive oil
2 onions, thinly sliced
1 garlic clove
2 x 400 g tins butter beans
juice of ½ lemon
1 heaped tbsp crème fraîche

1.   Heat 1 tbsp of olive oil in a large pan and sauté the onions and garlic until soft.
2.   Add the butter beans and one can of water. Cook until virtually all the liquid is incorporated.
3.   Blitz in the food processor until smooth. Add plenty of seasoning, lemon juice and crème fraiche and blend briefly.
4.   Transfer to a serving dish and keep warm until ready to serve.

This purée can be eaten in place of mash and makes a great nutritious topping to a cottage pie.

Chicken Supreme

Having discovered this in 1980, I have made it many times for guests. It is a bit like a chicken Kiev in that it has a crispy coating. It makes for a great light main course and most of the work is done in advance.

Serves 6

150 g soured cream
2 tbsp lemon juice
2 tsp Worcestershire sauce
1 level tsp garlic salt
1 level tsp celery salt
2 level tsp paprika
black pepper
6 boneless chicken breasts, skin removed
175 g fresh white breadcrumbs
6 tbsp finely chopped parsley
100 g butter
5 tbsp olive oil

1.   The day before you want to serve, place the soured cream, lemon juice, Worcestershire sauce, salts, paprika and pepper in a bowl and combine.
2.   Put the chicken breasts in a large shallow dish and pour over the cream sauce, turn the chicken breasts until they are evenly coated. Cover and refrigerate.
3.   Combine the breadcrumbs and parsley and place on a plate. Preheat the oven to 200/fan 180/gas 4.

4.   Melt the butter and combine with the oil. Pour⅔ in the base of a large roasting tin.

5.   Coat the chicken breasts evenly in the breadcrumbs pressing down with your fingers. Place the chicken on top of the butter and pour over the remaining oil and butter mix.

6.   Cook the chicken for 45 minutes until golden and crispy.

Serve on a spoonful of romesco sauce.

Lasagne

This recipe is the closest I can get to the creamy lasagnes I ate in a local Italian restaurant in the 1970s. Lasagne is so much easier to make now we no longer have to precook the lasagne sheets in boiling water. The whole lasagne can be frozen and then makes for a very easy supper with friends.

Serves 8

150 g butter
110 g plain flour
1.5 litres milk
150 ml double cream
grated nutmeg
1 quantity ragu (see page 65)
300 g fresh lasagne sheets or dried
100 g grated parmesan
salt and black pepper

1.   Preheat the oven to 160 fan/180/gas 4.
2.   Melt the butter in a very large saucepan. Stir in the flour and cook over a moderate heat for a couple of minutes. Slowly add the milk stirring all the time. Whisk then stir over a very low heat for ten minutes. Add the cream, one tsp grated nutmeg and seasoning.
3.   In a large ovenproof dish 24 x 32 cm, spread ¼ of the ragu and a large ladleful of the sauce. Top with lasagne sheets and repeat this process three more times. You need to finish with a layer of lasagne sheets and then a final good layer of sauce. Make sure you leave enough of the white sauce for this final layer. Cover with grated parmesan and bake for 45 minutes or until golden on top.

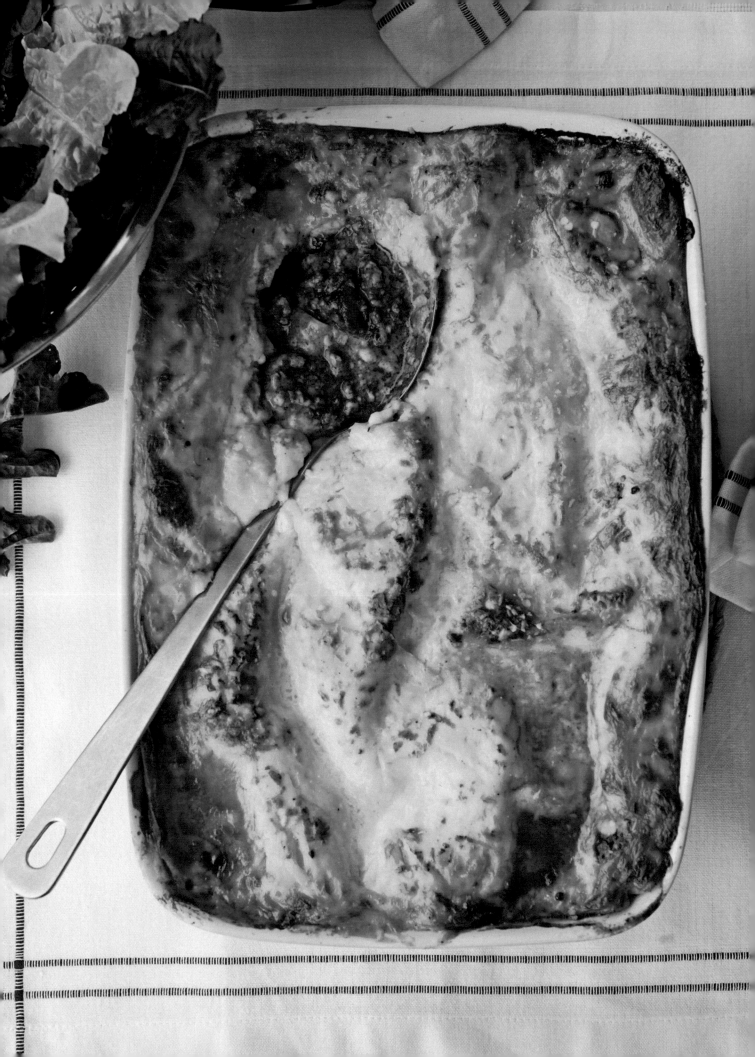

Beef with Stout and Pickled Walnuts

I used to make pickled onions and pickled red cabbage every year but have never made pickled walnuts. The walnuts add a tang to this rich beef casserole. This casserole looks after itself once you pop it in the oven and makes for a great family lunch after a bracing winter walk. You will get a better result if you marinate the meat overnight but if you are short of time a few hours will do.

3 kg stewing beef, cut into 3 cm squares
2 bay leaves
4 thyme sprigs
1.2 litres dark stout such as Guinness
250 ml port
85 g butter
3 tbsp olive oil
225 g onions, chopped
2 garlic cloves, peeled and crushed
2 x 400 g jars pickled walnuts
2 level tbsp of flour
salt and black pepper

1.   Place the meat in a large bowl along with the bay leaf and thyme. Pour over the stout and port, cover and leave overnight.

2.   The next day preheat the oven to 140/fan 120/gas 1. Drain the meat reserving the liquid and herbs. Dry by laying meat pieces on kitchen paper.

3.   Heat half the butter and oil and brown the meat in small quantities on a high heat before transferring to a large heatproof casserole.

4.   Add the rest of the butter and oil to the casserole. Cook the onion and garlic gently for about ten minutes until soft.

5.   Drain the walnuts and cut them into quarters.

6.   Stir the flour into the meat before adding the onions, walnuts, reserved liquid and herbs, and seasoning.

7.   Bring to a gentle simmer, cover and transfer to the oven. Cook for three hours.

Serve with creamy mash or dauphinoise potatoes with carrot batons and seasonal green vegetables.

Butternut and Goat's Cheese Tart

Rebecca found this recipe for me and we have used it as the vegetarian option at her children's naming celebrations and I have made it many times in the last nine years. Once cooked it freezes really well and makes one large 25 cm quiche. To reheat just wrap in foil and pop in a moderate oven for 20 minutes. If you do not have one large flan tin, use two smaller ones.

Serves 8

Pastry
125 g chilled butter, cubed
250 g plain flour
about 50 ml cold water
1 egg yolk

Filling
500 g butternut squash, peeled, deseeded and cut into 1cm cubes
1 onion, chopped
1 tbsp olive oil
250 ml double cream
250 ml single cream
3 eggs
2 tbsp grated parmesan
125 g soft goat's cheese
salt and black pepper

1.   Use a food processor to make the pastry or do this by hand. Rub the butter into the flour until it resembles fine breadcrumbs. Add the water and egg yolk to combine into a ball that leaves the sides of the bowl. Chill for 20 minutes.

2.   Preheat the oven to 180 fan/200/gas 6.

3.   Roll out the pastry and line a 23 cm flan tin. Ensure that the pastry is pushed into the edges of the tin and trim. Chill for 20 minutes.

4.   Place baking parchment in the tin over the pastry and fill with baking beans. Bake for 15 minutes, remove the beans and the parchment and bake for a further ten minutes.

5.   Mix the squash with the oil and roast on a tray lined with baking parchment in the oven for 15 minutes. Add the onion and cook for a further ten minutes.

6.   Beat the cream and eggs together and season well. Sprinkle the parmesan in the base of the tart, followed by the squash. Dot the goats cheese around evenly and pour over the egg mixture.

7.   Bake in the oven for 35–40 minutes until puffed and golden. Remove and serve warm or at room temperature.

Pepper Pissaladiere Tartlets

I have been told by my Uncle who lived in Paris that these tarts are as good as any tomato tart you can eat in France. They are perfect for a special summer lunch or supper and although there are a few elements all of them can be made in advance and just put together just before serving. This recipe makes 8 but the pastry cases can be made the day before so if you are feeding a crowd just make a couple of batches.

Serves 8

Pastry
150 g cold butter
1 teaspoon icing sugar
225 g plain flour
1 egg, separated
1 tsp lemon juice
2–3 tbsp cold water

Filling
4 tbsp olive oil
2 large onions, finely chopped
1 heaped tsp fresh oregano leaves (or dried)
1 x 400 g tin chopped tomatoes
140 g double concentrate tomato purée
1 large tsp fresh thyme leaves
1 tsp caster sugar
5 tbsp grated parmesan
50 g butter
salt and black pepper
pinch of crushed dried chillies

Garnish
1 red and 1 yellow pepper
olive oil
16 Greek-style black olives

1.   Make the pastry in a food processor or by hand. Rub the butter, icing sugar and flour until resembles fine breadcrumbs. Beat together the egg yolk, lemon juice and water and add to the flour and form the pastry into one ball. Wrap and chill in the fridge for one hour.

2.   Preheat the oven to 180 fan/200 gas 6. Place the peppers whole on a baking sheet, rub with oil and roast for 30 minutes.

3.   Put the roasted peppers in a bowl and cover for 30 minutes, before peeling and deseeding. Cut into thin strips and set aside.

4.   For the filling, melt the butter in a large saucepan. Cook the onions with the oregano for 15 minutes until transparent and very soft. Add the chopped tomatoes, tomato puree, thyme and sugar. Season and cook over a low heat for 20 minutes until you have a thick puree. Stir in three tbsp of the grated parmesan and leave to cool.

5.   Remove the pastry from the fridge ten minutes before you want to roll it out. Use eight individual fluted tart tins or one large 23 cm tart tin. Divide the pastry into eight and roll out to about 3mm. Line the tart tins, prick the base with a fork and refrigerate for 30 minutes.

6.   Place two baking sheets in the oven to preheat. Line the tarts with baking parchment and baking beans. Bake for ten minutes, remove the beans and paper then bake for a further five minutes, until the base is crisp and lightly browned. Remove from the oven and brush with the egg white.

7.   When ready to serve, assemble the tarts. Divide two tbsp of parmesan with a pinch of crushed chillies among the tarts. Top with equal amounts of the tomato mixture and finally the roasted red pepper strips and black olives. Brush with olive oil and scatter over some thyme leaves. Bake for 15 minutes. Serve warm.

6. My Life in the Kitchen
2000–2010

The new century seemed to revolutionise the outlook towards food and cooking at home. I became aware of cookery writers such as Nigella Lawson, Nigel Slater and Jamie Oliver. The focus was on good ingredients and simple kitchen suppers for friends. Gordon Ramsay provided recipes that required more time and skill but sometimes I wanted the distraction of a day in the kitchen.

Since I first decided to get a food processor over a stand mixer in the 1970s, I had always hankered after one. I got my first KMix in 2006 and it has made making cakes and meringues easier and nougat possible, but to my mind not an essential. In my personal life, I entered the new millennium with two teenagers to feed, they were not convinced by my vegetarian leanings, so I was still serving some meat. When they were not around, I am not proud to say I lived on pasta pesto. I was still entertaining but while I was on my own this was very much kitchen based and I always made sure I nominated a wine monitor to make my life easier. When, my now husband, Marc and I became partners I was bemused that he regarded cornflakes as a supper dish and never ate cake. It seemed rather a waste of my culinary talents, but it did not take long before he became used to a nutritious supper every night and an endless supply of cake in the tin.

We moved in together to a beautiful home with a very dodgy dingy kitchen. We managed to make it slightly bigger and install a farmhouse kitchen, but it remained a very small dark room.

In 2006, Vicki, my youngest daughter, became terminally ill and I struggled to work and care for her. She had some interesting food cravings whilst she endured gruelling treatment and my food bill rose to accommodate, lobster, smoked Salmon and sushi. Cooking for her was one of the ways I could show my love and care for her during a terrible time. I still have stickers in recipe books that she looked through to find food she fancied.

Vicki died in 2007 just 22 years old, we toast her at family meals and eat her favourite sticky toffee pudding in her memory.

Example weekly menus from 2000's

Sunday
Roasted vegetables with halloumi (recipe page 51)

Monday
Leek and broccoli bake

Tuesday
Mozzarella and aubergine pasta

Wednesday
Char grilled vegetables with couscous

Thursday
Feta and pine nut tarts with salad (recipe page 87)

Friday
Mushroom and spinach lasagne

Saturday, 16 April 2005 supper for friends
Cheese bites (recipe page 198)
Twice baked cauliflower soufflés (recipe page 100)
Roasted monkfish, mashed potatoes, green beans, mange tout
White chocolate tarts
Fruit salad

Sweet Things

Hazelnut Vacherin

This is a very impressive three-tier meringue dessert that can be filled with nectarines or raspberries in the summer or cubed mango in the winter. Well-drained tinned pears also work well. This is a great dessert to use up egg whites and to make in advance. Meringue was Martin's favourite dessert. I have always found meringues to be far too sweet and as a child would call individual meringues headache buns!

Serves 10

50 g toasted hazelnuts
6 egg whites
350 g caster sugar
600 ml double cream
6 ripe nectarines

1.   Place 3 x 23 cm silicone discs on baking trays and preheat the oven to 120 fan/140/gas1.
2.   Very finely chop the hazelnuts or blitz briefly in a food processor.
3.   In a clean dry bowl, whisk the egg whites until stiff, then whisk in the sugar 1tbsp at a time until stiff and glossy.
4.   Carefully stir in the nuts with a metal spoon.

5. Pipe or spread the meringue equally over the three discs. (This is easier if you use a small blob of the meringue to secure the disc to the baking sheet)

6. Bake in the oven for 60–75 minutes until crisp and dry. Leave to cool.

7. Whip the cream until fairly stiff. Stone and slice the nectarines. Remove the paper from the meringue discs and layer with the cream and fruit, finishing with a layer to top. Scatter over raspberries and hazelnuts if using.

The meringues can be stored for a least a week in a well-sealed plastic container.

Bakewell Tart

Over the years I have tried so many variations of Bakewell Tart and now have a whole folder of recipes for it. This is the best. I make my own raspberry jam but if you buy it make sure it is a good quality – it will make a difference.

Serves 12

Pastry
100 g butter
90 g icing sugar
1 egg and 2 egg yolks
250 g plain flour

Filling
250 g butter
250 g caster sugar
2 eggs
80 g plain flour
250 g ground almonds
finely grated zest of ½ lemon and juice of x lemon
1 tsp vanilla extract
250 g raspberry jam
40 g flaked almonds
4 tbsp apricot preserve

Icing
50 g icing sugar
1 tbsp lemon juice

1.   For the pastry, cream the butter and icing sugar together until pale and fluffy. Mix the egg and egg yolks together until incorporated then slowly beat into the sugar and butter. Add the flour and mix until a dough is formed. Depending on the size of your eggs you may need to add a tsp of water. Bring the dough together in a ball then cover and chill for 30 minutes.

2.   Roll out the chilled pastry to 3mm then line a 2 cm round x 3 cm deep tart tin. Press firmly into the tin and chill for a further hour. Remove from the fridge, check again that it is firmly in the tin, then prick the base and trim away any excess pastry.

3.   Preheat the oven to 180/160/gas 4. Line the pastry case with foil and fill with baking beans. Bake on a preheated baking sheet for 15 minutes, remove the beans and foil, then bake for a further ten minutes. Leave to cool.

4.   Spread the jam over the cooled tart case and place in the fridge.

5.   For the filling, cream the butter and sugar together until pale and fluffy. Add the eggs a little at a time, beating as you go. Sift the flour over the mixture, add the ground almonds, lemon zest and vanilla extract and fold in with a large metal spoon.

6.   Spoon the filling into the pastry case. It is easier to do this by placing spoonfuls around the case and bring them together rather than trying to spread all of it from the middle. Scatter over the flaked almonds and return to the hot baking sheet in the oven. Bake for 50 minutes until the filling is golden and set.

7.   Warm the apricot preserve with two tbsp of water and sieve. Brush onto the warm tart.

8.   Mix lemon juice with icing sugar to make a drizzling consistency and drizzle lines of it across the tart. Serve at room temperature.

Pear and Amaretti Cheesecake

Marc loves cheesecake but not with any gelatine. This is a lovely soft set cheesecake that requires no baking. An impressive dessert when served in individual ring moulds.

Serves 12

250 g digestive biscuits
125 g butter
2 x 400 g can pear halves (in juice, not syrup)
300 g full fat cream cheese
150 g caster sugar
½ tsp vanilla essence
300 ml double cream
150 g full fat crème fraîche
75 g crushed amaretti biscuits

1.   Finely crush the digestive biscuits. Melt butter and mix with the crumbs. Press firmly into the base of 12 individual ring moulds or 1 x 23 cm spring form tin. Chill.
2.   Drain 1 can of pears and chop into small dice. Leave to dry on kitchen paper.
3.   Mix together the cream cheese, sugar and vanilla until soft.

4.   Whip the cream and creme fraiche to a soft peak consistency and mix with the cream cheese. Add the chopped pears and amaretti biscuits.

5.   Pour the mixture over the biscuit mixture and refrigerate for at least four hours, preferably overnight.

6.   Run a knife around each mould and press out each cheesecake.

7.   Serve with additional drained pear cut into thin slices.

Chocolate Mousse

Over the years, I have made so many different recipes for chocolate mousse. This is definitely a winner and a much-shared recipe. Children and adults alike love the light and airy texture.

Serves 4

120 g dark chocolate
5 egg whites
40 g caster sugar
2 egg yolks

1.   Break the chocolate into pieces and place in a bowl. Set the bowl over a pan of boiling water, turn off the heat and do not let the bowl touch the water. Leave for several minutes, stirring occasionally until the chocolate is smooth.
2.   Whisk the egg white in a clean dry bowl until they form soft peaks. Add the caster sugar and whisk until firm peaks are formed.
3.   Stir the egg yolks into the melted chocolate.
4.   Whisk one third of the chocolate mixture into the egg whites then gently fold in the remaining two thirds.
5.   Pour the mousse into a serving bowl and refrigerate for at least four hours.

Apple and Nut Strudel

I used to make this pudding regularly as a teenager for our family Sunday lunch, before filo pastry was readily available to buy. Strudel pastry is quite relaxing to stretch out but very time consuming so I have adapted this to use pre-prepared pastry now it is easily available in all supermarkets.

100 g butter
85 g fresh white breadcrumbs
50 g walnuts or hazelnuts, roughly chopped
450 g cooking apples, peeled, cored and chopped
1 tsp ground cinnamon
50 g caster sugar
50 g sultanas
grated rind of ½ lemon
270 g filo pastry

1.   Preheat the oven to 220/fan 200/gas 7.
2.   Melt 50 g butter and gently fry the breadcrumbs until golden.
3.   Mix the cinnamon and sugar. Melt the remaining butter.
4.   Place sheets of filo pastry on baking parchment to measure 44 x 44 cm. Brush with melted butter and place a further 2 layers on top, ensuring each layer is brushed with butter.
5.   Leaving a border of 5 cm, spread over the breadcrumbs followed by the apple, nuts, sultanas and lemon zest . Finally, sprinkle over the cinnamon sugar.
6.   Turn the two side edges five cm and roll up the strudel. Using the baking parchment transfer to a baking tray and brush liberally with the remaining butter. Bake for 20 minutes until golden brown.

Serve warm with ice cream, custard or cream. Dust with icing sugar just before serving.

Individual Sticky Toffee Puddings

I first ate this pudding at the Sharrow Bay hotel in the Lake District in 1989 and have been making it ever since. Vicki loved this dessert so we always have it at Christmas and Easter in her memory. The grandchildren have come to love them too and even they manage to eat a whole one! Easy to make and freeze really well.

Serves 8

Puddings
75 g softened butter
175 g dried and pitted dates
175 ml boiling water
½ tsp vanilla essence
1 tsp instant coffee dissolved in 2 tsp boiling water
¾ tsp bicarbonate of soda
150 g caster sugar
2 eggs
175 g self-rising flour

Sauce
175 g brown sugar
110 g butter
6 tbsp double cream

1.   Preheat the oven to 180/fan 160/gas 4
2.   Grease and baseline with a disc of baking parchment 8 ovenproof mini pudding moulds or ramekins.

3.   Chop the dates and place in a bowl with the boiling water, vanilla, coffee and bicarbonate of soda. Leave to cool slightly.

4.   In a large mixing bowl, cream the butter and sugar together until light and fluffy. Beat the eggs together and add to the butter a little at a time, beating well after each addition.

5.   Carefully and lightly fold in the sifted flour then finally fold in the date mixture, including all the liquid.

6.   Divide the mixture equally among the 8 moulds or ramekins, place on a baking tray and bake in the oven for 25 minutes.

7.   When cool enough to handle, slide a small knife around each pudding and turn it out onto a baking tray, not forgetting to remove the disc of baking parchment.

8.   Place all the sauce ingredients in a small saucepan over a gentle heat, stir until the butter is melted and the sugar dissolved.

9.   To serve, pour one tbsp of the sauce over each pudding and return to the oven for ten minutes to warm through. Place the puddings on plates, pour over the remaining hot sauce and serve with lots of cream or ice cream.

These puddings freeze really well. Defrost and follow serving instructions.

Baked Alaska

I always hated Christmas pudding as a child, although I always had a piece, just in case I managed to get the hidden sixpence. Although I always made Christmas pudding, I quickly discovered my own children could not be persuaded to eat it. I therefore started the tradition 30 years ago of making a baked Alaska which seemed to be the perfect dessert to replicated the flaming Christmas pudding.

Sponge
65 g caster sugar
2 eggs
50 g plain white flour
1 extra tsp flour and caster sugar

Meringue
4 egg whites
225 g caster sugar
1 litre good-quality vanilla ice cream (not soft scoop)
small handful of flaked almonds (optional)

1.   Soften the ice cream then line a 18 cm deep tin with cling film. Spoon the ice cream into the tin, cover and freeze for at least three hours.
2.   Preheat the oven 180/fan 160/gas 4. Line a 20 cm loose based cake tin base lined with baking parchment. Grease the base and sides and tip in the tsp of flour and caster sugar and use to dust the tin.
3.   Whisk the eggs with caster sugar until pale and mousse like in texture. Sift in the flour and fold in gently. Pour into the prepared tin and bake for 25 minutes until the sponge is brown and firm to touch. Cool slightly before removing from the tin and placing on a wire rack.

4. When ready to serve preheat the oven to 230/fan 210/ gas 8.

5. Whisk the egg whites until they stand in soft peaks. Gradually whisk in the sugar one spoonful at a time, keeping the mixture stiff. (The meringue will keep in the fridge for two hours before using as instructed below.)

6. Place the sponge in a large glass ovenproof dish that is 2.5 cm bigger than the sponge. Place the ice cream on top and spoon the meringue all over the sponge cake and ice cream spreading it evenly over the surface. Build up the meringue into peaks ensuring there are no gaps.

7. Sprinkle over the flaked almonds and bake immediately for four minutes.

You can freeze the Alaska at the end of step 6 for two hours. Bake from frozen for 8 minutes in a 200/fan 180/gas 6 oven.

Chocolate Roulade

This recipe always pleases a crowd. There are lots of roulade recipes but this one has a lovely mousse-like texture so it will crack on rolling which I think adds to its appearance. It has the benefit of being gluten free. I first made this in 1983 and it has graced many a dinner party table since then.

Serves 6–8

175 g dark chocolate
3 tbsp hot water
5 eggs, separated
175 g caster sugar
300 ml double cream, whipped
Icing sugar for dusting

1.	Preheat the oven to 180/160 fan/gas mark 4. Line a 38 x 23 cm swiss roll tin with baking parchment.
2.	Break the chocolate into pieces and place in a bowl with the hot water. Set the bowl over a pan of boiling water, turn off the heat and do not let the bowl touch the water. Leave for several minutes, stirring occasionally until the chocolate is smooth.
3.	Whisk the egg yolks and sugar together until thick and pale (about ten minutes) then stir into the chocolate mixture.
4.	Whisk the egg whites until stiff, briskly fold 1 tablespoon into the chocolate mixture, then carefully fold in the remaining egg whites. Pour the mixture into the prepared tin and bake in the centre of a preheated oven for 15–20 minutes until firm.

5.   Cover with a sheet of baking parchment and then a slightly damp tea towel until cold.

6.   Turn out the roulade onto a large sheet of greaseproof paper dusted with icing sugar. Carefully remove the lining paper. Spread roulade with the whipped cream.

7.   With a serving plate ready, roll up the roulade from the shortest end using the greaseproof paper to help you roll. Place on the serving plate, dust with icing sugar and serve.

The roulade will keep in the fridge for several hours or even overnight although it may need an extra dusting of icing sugar before serving.

Ghirardelli Square Chocolate Ice Cream

I am not a great fan of ice-cream, but I am in the minority. This is a very smooth no churn recipe that was given to me by my friend Jill following a holiday to San Francisco in the late 1970s. Ghirardelli Square is the location of what was a famous chocolate factory.

Serves 6

200 g dark chocolate
4 tbsp cold water
50 g caster sugar
3 egg yolks
150 ml single cream
150 ml double cream

1.   Grate the chocolate and put in the blender of a food processor.
2.   Bring the water to the boil, stir in the sugar and dissolve completely. Return to boiling point then simmer for five minutes.
3.   Pour the syrup onto the grated chocolate and blend until completely smooth, adding a drop more hot water if necessary.
4.   Lightly whisk the egg yolks, add to the chocolate and blend again.
5.   Whisk the two creams together until thickened but not stiff. Gently stir into the chocolate mixture until combined.
6.   Freeze overnight. Remove from freezer 20 minutes before serving.

Shortbread and Raspberry Stacks

I discovered this recipe in 1995 and continue to use it to this day because it is a special dessert that can be served to lots of guests. I have used this to feed 135 people at a party and although I was rather fed up with making the shortbread discs it was so easy to assemble and serve. The combination of buttery shortbread with cream and raspberries makes a decedent summer dessert. To make it less rich use half whipped cream mixed with the same quantity of Greek yoghurt.

Serves 6

Shortbread
50 g icing sugar
100 g very soft butter
135 g plain flour
1 egg yolk

Raspberry sauce
250 g fresh raspberries
40 g caster sugar
2 tsp lemon juice
To serve
300 ml double cream
300 g fresh raspberries
icing sugar

1.   In a bowl mix the icing sugar, egg yolk and butter and add the flour rub together then combine until you have a soft dough. (You can do this in a food processor.) Bring the dough together, wrap and chill for two hours.

2.   Place the raspberries for the sauce in a bowl with the caster sugar and lemon juice. Leave for 1 hour. Sieve to extract as much puree as possible and set aside in the fridge

3.   Preheat the oven 140 fan/160/gas 3. Roll the pastry out thinly and cut into 12 discs using a plain or fluted 9 cm cutter. Place on a parchment-lined baking tray and bake for 10–15 minutes until pale blonde. Remove from the oven and allow to cool on a wire rack.

4.   Whip the cream until it holds its shape. Place the cream and raspberries on half the shortbread rounds, top with a second shortbread round and dust with icing sugar. To serve each shortbread with a puddle of raspberry sauce.

The shortbread rounds keep well for several days in an airtight container. The raspberry sauce can be made a day ahead and kept in the fridge.

Lemon Posset

This is a great dessert for a crowd, just increase the quantities. Tasty and refreshing, you can make it a couple of days ahead. The posset as we know it with cream and lemons originates from the sixteenth century. I have been making this for 25 years and it always gets lots of compliments.

Serves 6

600 ml double cream
150 g caster sugar
Zest and juice of 2 large lemons

1.   Place the cream and sugar in a pan and carefully bring to the boil, stirring slowly. Simmer for a few minutes then add the lemon zest and juice. Stir well.
2.   Pour the mixture into six glasses. Chill for at least four hours.

This is delicious on its own, but you can serve it with a few raspberries and a slice of shortbread or even a teaspoon of cassis on top.

Lemon Syrup Tart

I love to make this dessert at Easter as a change from all the chocolate around. The golden syrup gives this a very smooth texture.

Serves 8

Pastry
125 g butter
225 g plain flour

Filling
225 g golden syrup
50 g butter
300 ml double cream
150 ml soured cream
3 eggs
1 lemon

Preheat the oven to 200/180 fan/gas mark 6.

1.   Place the butter and flour in a food processor and process until it resembles fine breadcrumbs (or rub by hand). Add cold water, one tbsp at a time, until you have a soft dough. Knead very lightly to bring it together then wrap and chill for 30 minutes.
2.   Roll out the pastry and use to line a 23 cm deep, loose-based fluted flan tin. Chill again for ten minutes.

3. Line the tart with non-stick baking parchment and fill with baking beans. Bake blind at 200 fan/180 for 20 minutes. Remove the baking beans and parchment and bake for a further 8–10 minutes until the pastry is well dried out. Reduce the oven temperature to 180 fan/160.

4. In a saucepan melt the golden syrup and butter together over a gentle heat. In a separate bowl, whisk the creams, eggs, grated lemon rind and two tbsp of lemon juice. Combine with the syrup and butter mixture and pour into the pastry case.

5. Bake for about 45 minutes at 180 fan/160 until the top is set but the filling wobbles slightly in the centre.

6. Serve warm or at room temperature on its own or with red berries.

Whole Orange and Almond Cake

I first made this recipe in the 1990s and it became a firm favourite because it is easy, tasty and freezes well. In recent years it has also been useful in providing a delicious gluten free cake or dessert. I serve this as a dessert with Greek yoghurt and oranges in caramel. You will make more than you need but the flavours do not work as well if you try to cut down the quantities. So, freeze a cake and have an easy dessert to hand.

Makes 3 loaf cakes or 1 loaf cake and one 20 cm loose bottomed cake tin

3 whole oranges
9 medium eggs
350 g ground almonds
350 g caster sugar
½ tsp baking powder

1.   Line three cake tins with baking parchment.
2.   Wash the oranges and place them in a saucepan, cover with cold water and bring to a simmer. Simmer for one hour. Remove from the water, quarter the oranges and drain well. Remove the pips and blitz to a puree, using a food processor or liquidiser. Leave to cool.
3.   Preheat the oven to 160 fan/180/gas 4.

4.   Whisk the egg whites until they are thick and leave a trail when the whisk is lifted. Mix together the almonds, sugar and baking powder then fold into the egg mixture. Carefully add the orange puree then pour the cake mixture equally into the 3 loaf tins. (If using the 20 cm tin place one third in a loaf tin and two thirds in the cake tin.)

5.   Bake for 40–45 minutes until firm and pierced with a knife it comes out clean. If cooking a 20 cm cake it will take about an hour. Remove from the oven to cool. The cake may sink slightly when cooled.

Oranges in Caramel

I have been making this recipe since the 1970s and it still gets compliments today. Although we are all trying to reduce our sugar consumption, just a small amount of the caramel sauce is a real treat. This is very easy to prepare and will sit happily in the fridge for a couple of days. Bring to room temperature before serving. Great served with whole orange cake recipe for a lactose and gluten free dessert.

Serves 6

4 large oranges
240 g sugar
300 ml water

1.   Carefully pare the outer rind of two oranges with vegetable peeler. Cut into thin matchstick strips. Put in small bowl and cover with boiling water.
2.   Peel the two remaining oranges, removing any pith and cut into round slices. Remove any pips and place slices with any juices into a shallow serving bowl.
3.   Place all the sugar and 150 ml water into a saucepan and dissolve the sugar over a low heat. When dissolved, increase the heat and boil rapidly until it turns a rich caramel brown colour. Remove from the heat and pour in the remaining water, being careful of any splashing. Return to a low heat and stir until all the caramel is dissolved.
4.   Cool the caramel sauce then pour over oranges. Drain and dry the orange rind and sprinkle over the oranges.

Tiramisu

I have always loved tiramisu and in the late 90s would buy individual shop-bought tiramisu to cheer myself up. This is in a different league. Marc always swore he hated tiramisu until he ate this without realising what it was, it is now one of his 'favourites'. You will have a lot of egg whites left over so if you are having friends around, make a hazelnut vacherin (see page 135) as a second dessert.

Serves 8 generously

6 egg yolks
100 g sugar
150 ml marsala
500 g mascarpone
250 ml strong coffee (good quality instant will do)
1 packet sponge fingers
cocoa powder

1.   Place the egg yolks and sugar in a bowl set over a pan of barely simmering water. Whisk with an electric whisk for 3–4 minutes until pale and very thick. Remove from the heat, whisk in 100 ml marsala and continue to whisk for 5 minutes. In a separate bowl whisk the mascarpone to soften then whisk this into the marsala mix.
2.   Mix the remaining 50 ml of marsala with the coffee, dip in each sponge finger and line the base of a deep serving dish approx. 28 x 16 or 1.5 litres in volume. Spoon over one third of the mascarpone mixture and dust with cocoa. Repeat this with two more layers finishing with a layer of mascarpone and a dusting of cocoa. Chill overnight or for a minimum of four hours before serving.

Raspberry and White Chocolate Trifle

I love a trifle and we are lucky enough to grow our own raspberries. I make sure I freeze some so we can enjoy this summery trifle for dessert on a gloomy winter's day. It is a very different type of trifle to the ones I used to make in the 1970s that included jelly, tinned fruit and bird's custard.

Serves 8-10

750 g frozen raspberries
100 g caster sugar
250 g cantuccini biscuits
6 tbsp dessert wine
200 g white chocolate
500 g fresh custard
450 ml double cream
500 ml crème fraîche
1 tbsp caster sugar
50 g toasted flaked almonds (optional)

1.   Remove the cream, custard and crème fraîche from the fridge.
2.   Place the raspberries in a pan over a low heat with the sugar. Heat until the sugar has dissolved and the fruit is thawed.

3.   Strain the fruit in a sieve over a bowl to catch the juices. Leave to cool. Return the juice to the pan, simmer for about ten minutes until reduced to about 150 ml.

4.   Lay the cantuccini biscuits in a large glass trifle bowl. Spoon over the wine, followed by the fruit.

5.   Put the chocolate in a bowl set over barely simmering water. Stir until melted, remove from the heat and cool slightly before folding in the custard a little at a time.

6.   Whip the cream lightly and reserve half. Fold the remaining cream into the custard mixture and then use this to cover the fruit.

7.   Beat the crème fraîche until smooth then fold in the reserved cream together with one tbsp of caster sugar. Use this to cover the custard. Chill for at least two hours.

8.   If using, sprinkle toasted almonds over the trifle just before serving.

Truffle Torte

It would be hard for me to choose just one recipe book but near the top of the list would be Delia Smith's Christmas. I have followed her instructions for cooking Christmas lunch ever since it was first published in 1990. This is a wonderfully easy chocolate dessert that tastes delicious and is impossible to improve on. It freezes really well and is easy to transport when taking a pudding contribution to others. Beware – it is very rich!

Serves 10

75 g crunchy Amaretti biscuits
450 g dark chocolate
5 tbsp liquid glucose
5 tbsp rum
600 ml double cream
23 cm springform tin lined on the base and sides with baking parchment

1.   Crush the Amaretti biscuits finely and sprinkle over the base of the tin.
2.   Break up the chocolate and put into a bowl with the liquid glucose and rum. Set over a pan of barely simmering water and leave until the chocolate has melted and is smooth. Stir from time to time. Cool until just warm.
3.   In a separate bowl beat the cream until slightly thickened, do not over whisk. Fold half the mixture into the chocolate mixture until well blended. Fold into the rest of the cream. When it is smoothly blended, pour into the prepared tin.
4.   Cover and chill overnight. Prior to serving, remove from the tin and remove the sidelining paper. Place a serving plate on top of the torte and flip over. Remove the base of the tin and paper. Dust with cocoa and serve with softly whipped cream.

7. My Life in the Kitchen
2010–2020

It seems that this is the era of food. So much awareness of food and so many new ingredients available. Vegan has become the new vegetarian and almost everyone has a dietary requirement of one sort or another. After entertaining for over 40 years, supper parties have become much harder to plan. Generally, I will still cook meat if I am entertaining but often there is a vegetarian dish as well.

In 2012, I cooked my first Yotam Ottolenghi recipe and from then on, I was hooked. I love the Middle Eastern influence and the fresh flavours. Recipes seem to be everywhere from weekend supplements to new cookery books and supermarket magazines. Not all the new ideas are a success, a cauliflower pizza base is no match for the real thing, however, Yotam Ottolenghi's cauliflower cake is a firm favourite.

During this time, the three grandchildren, Holly, Rosie and Jack, who arrived in 2011, 2013 and 2015 mean I have to go back to child-friendly cooking. Their favourite is cheesy pasta made with Granny's easy tomato sauce. However, the standard of cake decoration has declined, three children, one chocolate fudge cake, sweets and chocolates make for rather 'fun' results.

As a coffee lover, my top appliance of the decade is my Nespresso coffee machine. For the first time, I can make better coffee at home than I can get out. I have dabbled with a spiraliser, fun but not an essential bit of kit. In this decade, I finally acquired the kitchen of my dreams. Everything I have learnt about what is needed in a functioning kitchen was put into place. The only fancy appliance is a boiling water tap, brilliant, no kettle on the worktop or to breakdown. Apart from that, the kitchen is very simple, but the pan and crockery drawers have revolutionised Marc's life – he no longer has to bend down!

During this time, Marc and I are both very lucky to have retired and have the time to keep on top of the garden as well as travelling. We have also baked, run, walked, trekked, cycled, swum and generally sweated our way to raising nearly £44,000, including gift aid, for the Macmillan Vicki Cole tribute fund, set up in Vicki's memory.

Example weekly menus from 2010's

Saturday
Figs with labneh
Chard and Ricotta tart with mixed salad

Sunday
Cauliflower cake, baked potato, tender stem broccoli

Monday
Gnocchi with tomato sauce (recipe page 48)

Tuesday
Squash and goat's cheese gratin (recipe page 80)

Wednesday
Vegetable paella

Thursday
Mushroom and pearl barley risotto

Friday, 17 May 2019 – Helen's 60th Birthday Supper for Family
Cheese bites (recipe page 198)
Asparagus
Confit Duck (recipe page 105)
Dauphinoise potatoes, crushed peas, broccoli
Raspberry shortbread stacks (recipe page 152)

Baking

Amy's Chocolate Brownies

There are so many recipes for chocolate brownies, these really are the best. I made these for a party of 100 people and served them with tubs of ice cream and strawberries. I was asked for the recipe by at least ten people after that so they must be good. They freeze well. A big thank you to Amy for sharing the recipe.

Makes 12

200 g butter, chopped
400 g good-quality dark chocolate, broken
4 medium-large eggs
300 g light muscovado sugar
40 g ground almonds
80 g plain flour
1 tbsp cocoa powder, sifted

1.   Grease a 21 cm square tin and line with baking paper. Preheat the oven to 140 fan/160/gas 3.
2.   Add the butter and 300 g chocolate to a bowl and set over a pan of barely simmering water to melt, stirring occasionally. Once melted and combined, remove from the heat and set aside. Chop the remaining 100 g of chocolate.
3.   Add the eggs and sugar to a bowl and beat with an electric whisk for five minutes until thick and pale.
4.   Gently fold in the melted chocolate mixture then the ground almonds, flour, cocoa powder and remaining chocolate until combined.
5.   Tip the mixture into the prepared tin, gently tilting the pan tin to level the mixture.
6.   Bake for 45 minutes, or until just set, then remove from the oven and cool completely before cutting into 12 squares.

Carrot and Walnut Cake

I love carrot cake and have tried so many recipes, I thought I had found the best until I discovered this one by Yotam Ottolenghi. This is a light cake with the perfect amount of cream cheese frosting – delicious!

Serves 6–8

Cake
160 g plain flour
½tsp baking powder
½tsp bicarbonate of soda
1 tsp ground cinnamon
1 egg, 2 egg whites, 1 egg yolk
200 g sunflower oil
270 g caster sugar
50 g walnut halves, chopped
50 g desiccated coconut
2 carrots, peeled and grated to give 135 g
Salt

Topping
200 g cream cheese at room temperature
70 g very soft butter
35 g icing sugar
25 g honey
30 g walnut pieces, chopped and lightly toasted (optional)

1.   Preheat the oven to 170 fan/190/gas 5. Grease a 20 cm loose-bottomed cake tin and line the base and sides with baking parchment.

2.   Sift together the flour, baking powder and bicarbonate of soda. Lightly whisk in the one whole egg and one egg yolk.

3.   Put the sunflower oil and caster sugar in a large bowl of an electric mixer. Beat together for about one minute then on a low speed add the beaten egg. Mix in the walnuts, coconut and carrot then add the dry ingredients, being careful to not over mix.

4.   In a separate bowl, whisk the two egg whites with a pinch of salt until firm peaks are formed. Gently fold the egg white mixture into the carrot mixture in three additions, again being careful to not over mix.

5.   Carefully pour the mixture into the prepared tin and bake for one hour or until a skewer inserted into the middle comes out clean. Cool completely before removing from the tin.

6.   For the topping, beat the cream cheese with an electric mixer until light and smooth. In a separate bowl, beat together the butter, icing sugar and honey until light and airy. Fold the two mixtures together. Spread on top of the cake and sprinkle with nuts if using.

Chocolate Cupcakes with Chocolate Frosting

I do not think I had ever heard of cupcakes until after the turn of the new century. When I was a child, we made fairy cakes which were smaller and decorated with glace icing and this is what I made with my own children. Now I am rather partial to a cupcake although I prefer a cream cheese frosting to huge quantities of buttercream.

Makes 16

3 eggs
250 g caster sugar
½ tsp vanilla essence
50 g butter
100 ml sour cream
2 tbsp cold coffee
250 g plain flour
2 tsp baking powder
4 tbsp cocoa powder
100 g plain chocolate, melted

Frosting
60 g softened butter
300 g icing sugar
½ tsp vanilla essence
2 tbsp cocoa powder
100 g cream cheese
½ tbsp hot coffee

1. Preheat the oven to 160 fan/180/gas 4. Place 16 muffin cases in muffin tins.
2. In a large bowl beat the eggs and caster sugar together until thick, white and fluffy.
3. Melt the butter and mix with the sour cream, cold coffee and vanilla essence and fold into the creamed mixture.
4. Sieve the flour, baking powder and cocoa together and fold into the egg mixture with the melted chocolate.
5. Spoon equal amounts into the paper cases so they are about two thirds full.
6. Bake for 15–20 minutes until well risen. Remove from the oven and cool on a wire rack.
7. To make the frosting, mix together the butter, icing sugar, vanilla essence, cocoa powder and cream cheese in a bowl then stir in the hot coffee. Spread or pipe the frosting on top of the cold cupcakes.

Chocolate Fudge Cake

Who does not love a piece of chocolate cake? The grandchildren love both decorating and eating this lovely moist cake. I let them go mad with Maltesers, chocolate buttons and Smarties or mini chocolate eggs at Easter, but really this cake does not need any adornment.

50 g sifted cocoa powder
6 tbsp boiling water
3 eggs
50 ml milk
175 g self-raising flour
1 rounded tsp baking powder
100 g softened butter
275 g caster sugar

Topping and filling
150 g plain chocolate
150 ml double cream
3 tbsp apricot jam

1.   Preheat the oven 160 fan/ 180/gas 4. Grease and base line with parchment 2 x 20 cm sandwich tins.
2.   Mix the cocoa powder and boiling water in a large bowl. Add the remaining cake ingredients and beat until the mixture is a smooth, thick batter. Divide between the two tins and level the surface.
3.   Bake in the oven for 25–30 minutes, or until well risen and the tops spring back when lightly pressed. Once cool enough to handle, remove the cakes from the tin, peel off the parchment and leave to cool on a wire rack.

4.   For the icing, break the chocolate into pieces. Place in a bowl with the cream and set over a pan of barely simmering water. Heat until the chocolate melts, stirring occasionally. This will take about ten minutes. Once smooth, leave to cool until just starting to set.

5.   Warm the apricot jam. Sieve then spread a little over the base of one cake and the top of the other. Spread the chocolate mixture over the apricot on both cakes and sandwich together, smoothing the top.

Lemon Drizzle Cake

This is the cake I make when I want to make a cake in a hurry. You do not even have to ice it and it will still be delicious.

Makes 1

125 g softened butter
175 g caster sugar
2 eggs
Zest of 2 lemons
¼ tsp vanilla extract
175 g self-raising flour
Salt
3 tbsp milk (preferably full cream)

Lemon syrup
Juice of 2 lemons
100 g icing sugar

Icing
150 g sieved icing sugar
2 tbsp lemon juice

1.   Preheat the oven to 160 fan/180 gas 4. Line a 2 lb/900 g loaf tin – I use pre-formed parchment loaf tin liners; they make this job much easier.
2.   Beat the butter and sugar until light and fluffy. Add the eggs one at a time, beating well after each addition. Stir in the lemon zest and vanilla extract.

3.   Sift in the flour with a pinch of salt and fold gently until thoroughly combined. Stir in the milk.

4.   Pour into the prepared tin and bake for 40–50 minutes until a cake tester or skewer inserted in the middle comes out clean.

5.   Make the syrup by placing the lemon juice and icing sugar in a small pan over a low heat. Stir until the sugar has dissolved.

6.   When the cake is removed from the oven, pierce all over the surface with a skewer. Pour over the lemon syrup and leave to cool in the tin.

7.   Make the icing by mixing together the icing sugar and lemon juice. Remove the cake from the tin and remove the baking parchment. Spoon the icing over the cake letting it run down the sides.

Mincemeat and Marzipan Cake

This is more of a tea bread than a cake. If you use a food processor this cake can be made in a matter of minutes. It does require you to have some mincemeat in the cupboard but I find there are very few weeks of the year when mincemeat is not available to buy. Stock up with a couple of jars at Christmas and this tasty treat can be an easy standby when you want to rustle up a cake in super quick time. I make no apology for there being two cakes with marzipan in, included in this book I have always loved it ever since I made marzipan fruits every Christmas as a child.

200 g self-raising flour
100 g cold butter, cubed
85 g light muscovado sugar
85 g marzipan, cut into cubes
2 eggs
300 g mincemeat
2 tbsp flaked almonds

1.   Preheat the oven to 160 fan/180/gas 4. Line a 2lb/900 g loaf tin.
2.   Place the flour and butter in a food processor and blitz until you have fine crumbs (or do this by hand). Add the sugar and combine again. Transfer to a large bowl and stir in the included cubes.
3.   Stir the eggs into the mincemeat until well combined then add this to the flour mixture.
4.   Transfer to the prepared tin, smooth the top and sprinkle over the flaked almonds. Bake for one hour or until a skewer inserted comes out clean.
5.   Cool for ten minutes before removing from the tin and allowing to cool completely on a wire rack.

Walnut and Mixed Fruit Cake

This is a wonderful light fruit cake with lots of nuts and marzipan, one of my favourite combinations. I always make this when we go to the Lake District for a week, a couple of slices of this and a flask of coffee is an essential bit of kit when we are out walking in the hills.

125 g dried apricots
100 g natural glace cherries
150 g walnut pieces
125 g marzipan
250 g sultanas
2 medium oranges
175 g softened butter
175 g caster sugar
3 large eggs
250 g plain flour
1 tsp baking powder
1 tsp ground cinnamon

1.   Preheat the oven to 140 fan/160/gas 3. Line a 20 cm cake tin with baking parchment.
2.   Roughly chop the apricots, half the cherries and chop any large walnut pieces. Cut the marzipan into 2 cm squares and roll into balls. Grate the zest from the oranges and squeeze about 100 ml of the juice. Set all these ingredients aside.
3.   In a large bowl, using an electric mixer, cream the butter and sugar together until light and fluffy. Gradually beat in the eggs one at a time, adding a heaped tsp of the flour with each egg.

4.   Add the sultanas, walnuts, marzipan, apricots, cherries, orange zest and juice. Sift in the remaining flour, baking powder and cinnamon and stir gently until combined.

5.   Spoon into the prepared tin and level the top before placing in the oven for one hour.

6.   Reduce the oven temperature to 150/fan130/gas 2. Bake for a further hour until a cake tester or skewer comes out clean. You may need to bake for a further 10–15 minutes.

7.   Leave the cake to cool for half an hour in the tin before removing and leaving to cool completely.

This cake will keep well for a couple of weeks in an airtight container.

Mars Bar Squares

I discovered a version of this recipe in 1996. It tastes healthy but once you read the ingredients you will quickly realise it is not. It is delicious but one square is definitely enough. When I first started making this, there was one size of Mars bar. Now there are so many different sizes. I have given the weight required.

Makes 16

125 g Mars bars
150 ml double cream
225 g plain flour
110 g oats
150 g light muscovado sugar
½ tsp bicarbonate of soda
150 g butter, cubed
1 egg

1.   Preheat the oven to 160 fan/180/gas 4. Line a 24 cm square baking tin with baking parchment.
2.   Chop the Mars bars and add to a pan set over a low heat with the cream. Leave to melt, stirring occasionally.
3.   Place the flour, oats, sugar and bicarbonate of soda in a food processor. Process together before adding the cubed butter. Process until the mixture is combined and looks like fine breadcrumbs. Beat the egg and add before processing for a few seconds more.

4.   Press ¾ of the oat mixture into the prepared tin. Spread the Mars bar mixture on top before sprinkling with the remaining oat mixture.
5.   Bake in the oven for 25 minutes or until golden brown. Leave to cool for 30 minutes before cutting into squares.

These squares will keep in an airtight container for five days.

Easy Mince Pies

Most people say these do not taste anything like the mince pies they usually eat. The pastry resembles shortbread. They freeze extremely well and can be cooked from frozen, just give them an extra few minutes of cooking time. I have been making mince pies this way for 18 years now.

Makes 18

225 g cold butter, cubed
350 g plain flour
100 g caster sugar
1 jar of mincemeat

1.   Preheat the oven to 180 fan/200/gas 6.
2.   Place the butter, flour and sugar in a food processor and process until beginning to form a ball. This can be done by hand using the rubbing method.
3.   Transfer the mixture to a large bowl and bring together with your hands. (This mixture does not require any liquid and it will be quite firm. Do not chill it as it makes it difficult to handle.)
4.   Roll out the dough between two sheets of cling film to about 3mm. Do not worry if you cannot roll it out in one go. Just cut out rounds using a 7 cm plain pastry cutter for the base and 6 cm cutter for the lids. Re-roll the pastry until you have 18 bases and 18 lids. The pastry is very tolerant of being handled so don't worry if you have to re-roll is several times.
5.   Grease 18 holes of 2 x 12-hole pastry tins. Press the bases into the pastry tin, resealing any cracks that appear. Fill the pies with mincemeat. Dampen the edges of the lids with water and press gently onto the bases at the edges. They do not need to be too firmly sealed.
6.   Bake for 20 minutes until golden. Cool in the tins for ten minutes before transferring to a wire rack.
7.   The mince pies will keep for three to four days in an airtight container.

Buttermilk Scones

I have been making scones since I was young. The plethora of recipes is confusing but if you want a sweet fruit scone this recipe is hard to beat. They are not quite the same after they have been frozen, but I make double the quantity and keep a stash in the freezer and defrost one (a minute on defrost setting in the microwave) to go with my morning coffee. When they are fresh, it is hard to stop at one…

Makes 7–8 large scones

240 g self-raising flour
2 tsp baking powder
40 g caster sugar
60 g chilled butter
60 g raisins
175 ml buttermilk or 90 ml full fat milk mixed with 90 ml natural yoghurt
pinch of salt
1 egg yolk for brushing

1.   Preheat the oven to 170 fan/190/gas 3. Line a baking tray with baking parchment.
2.   Place the flour, baking powder and sugar in a food processor. Cube the butter, add to the mixture and process briefly until you have coarse grains. You can do this by hand using the rubbing in method.
3.   Place the scone mix in a large bowl and add the raisins, buttermilk and salt. Bring the dough together but do not overwork it. Leave to rest for five minutes.
4.   Roll out the dough on a floured work surface until it is 2.5 cm thick. Cut out the scones with a plain round 5 cm pastry cutter. Brush with the egg yolk.
5.   Bake for 20–25 minutes until risen and golden. Remove from the oven and place on a wire rack to cool.

Serve with butter and jam or jam and cream

Meringue Mice

I have been making these white mice since 1990, they proved very popular with all my nephews and nieces and they expected them every Christmas when all the family came to stay. Now I make them occasionally for the grandchildren.

Makes approximately 24

2 egg whites
125 g caster sugar
flaked almonds
edible silver balls
strawberry laces

1.   Preheat the oven to 90 fan/110/gas ¼.
2.   Whisk the egg whites until very stiff. Add the caster sugar 1 tbsp at a time, whisking well after each addition until very thick.
3.   Spoon the mixture into a large piping bag fitted with a 1 cm plain nozzle.
4.   Line a large tray with baking parchment. Pipe the mixture into mice shapes, with mounds at one end then tapering off at the other. Place one flaked almond for each ear and silver balls for the eyes and nose.
5.   Bake for two hours. When cool, remove from the tray and make a small hole at the tail end of each mouse and insert a length of the laces to form a tail.

These mice store well in an airtight tin for a week. Add the tails before serving or even serve 'manx' mice!

Shortbread

I have been making this lovely buttery shortbread for over 40 years and it still gets compliments. I tend to make a double batch as it keeps well for well over a week in an airtight tin.

Makes 8 pieces

150 g flour
30 g ground rice or rice flour
50 g caster sugar plus extra for sprinkling
115 g chilled butter, cut into cubes

1.   Place all the ingredients in a food processor and mix until it only just begins to come together. Transfer to a large bowl and bring together to form a ball, being careful not to overwork it.
2.   Place the dough on a sheet of baking parchment. Lightly roll out before pressing into a 18 cm fluted edged flan ring. Prick all over with a fork. Remove the flan ring and refrigerate for 30 minutes.
3.   Preheat the oven 140 fan/160/gas 3. Bake for 35-40 minutes or until pale golden. If you like a much crispier texture you may want to bake for a few minutes more.
4.   Remove from the oven, sprinkle with caster sugar then cut into eight pieces while still warm. Leave to cool on a wire rack before storing in an airtight tin.

Almond Petit Fours

I have been making these since the mid-1970s as a Christmas treat, that is before I discovered how great they are dipped in chocolate fondue. They make a super little treat for anyone who is gluten or lactose intolerant.

Makes approx. 24

2 egg whites
115 g ground almonds
60 g caster sugar
almond extract
glace cherries (optional)

1.   Preheat the oven to 160 fan/180/gas 4. Line two large baking sheets with baking parchment.
2.   Whisk the egg whites until stiff then fold in the almonds, sugar and just a few drops of almond extract.
3.   Spoon the mixture into a large piping bag fitted with a large star piping nozzle.
4.   Pipe out small rosettes onto the baking sheets. Top with a sliver of glace cherry if using. Bake in the oven for about 20 minutes, or until golden brown.
5.   Remove from the tray and leave to cool on a wire rack.

Chocolate Bites

I remember when Matchmakers were introduced in the late 1960s, those and After Eights were the only after dinner offer with coffee until pretty much the 1990s. Now most people still like a small chocolate after a meal, but unlike me less and less are drinking coffee. These go well with whatever you decide to drink and are so easy to make, the grandchildren can make them. They are a lovely gift too.

Makes 32

200 g dark, milk or white chocolate or use 70 g of each
120 g nut and dried fruit selection (pre-mixed bags are available)

1.   Take a large sheet of baking parchment and draw 32 x 5 cm circles. Turn the parchment over.
2.   Break the chocolate into a heatproof bowl. If you are using more than one type of chocolate, use separate bowls. Set over a pan of barely simmering water, making sure the base does not touch the water. Leave for a couple of minutes then stir until melted.
3.   Place about one tsp of chocolate into the centre of a circle. Place a few nuts and fruit onto the chocolate and use them to push the chocolate to the edges of the circle. Repeat.
4.   Leave to set then remove from the paper and store in an airtight tin in a cool place.

Some honey roasted nuts in the mix are nice too.

Nougat

You do need to love someone to make this for them. If you are a nougat lover, this is a real treat. I make it for Marc as a love token at Christmas, his birthday, Valentine's Day and Easter. You will need a stand mixer and a sugar thermometer. Rice paper is readily available on the internet.

150 g blanched almonds and 150 g hazelnuts
100 g pistachios
225 g granulated sugar
140 g clear honey
1½ tbsp liquid glucose
2 egg whites
1tsp vanilla extract

1.   Preheat the oven to 160 fan/ 180/ gas 4. Toast the almonds and hazelnut for 10 minutes. Line the base and sides of a 24 cm square tin and cut a piece of rice paper to fit the top later in the method.
2.   Roughly chop all the nuts. Reduce the oven temperature to 100/fan 80/gas 0.25.
3.   Place the nuts on a baking sheet and return to the warm oven.
4.   Place the sugar, liquid glucose, honey and 110 ml water in a pan set over a low heat. Stir until the sugar has dissolved.
5.   Turn up the heat and boil rapidly, monitoring the temperature. Whisk the egg whites in a stand mixer until they form soft peaks.

6.   When the sugar syrup reaches 160 degrees, slowly in a steady stream pour the syrup onto the egg whites, keeping the mixer whisking the whole time. Once all the syrup has been added, continue to whisk until the mixture is extremely thick and the machine struggles to continue!

7.   Add the warm nuts and vanilla extract and stir in by hand. Spoon into the prepared tin, level and place rice paper on top and press down. Cover with greaseproof paper, put another tin on top of this and place several tins of tomatoes or beans on top of this to weigh it down. Cool completely.

8.   Cut into bite-sized squares (a hot knife makes this easier) and store in an airtight tin for up to two weeks.

Cheese Bites

I have been making these for 25 years and they are great for nibbles before supper. Another recipe that I have already shared many times. They keep for up to a week in an airtight tin and the cheesy flavour improves over a couple of days.

150 g chilled butter, cubed
150 g self-raising flour
50 g stilton cheese
50 g cheddar cheese, grated
salt and cayenne pepper
1 level tbsp poppy seeds (optional)

1.   Place the butter, flour, stilton and cheddar in a food processor with a good pinch of salt and cayenne pepper. Blitz until the mixture comes together as a ball. Wrap and chill for 30 minutes.
2.   Roll out the pastry to 5mm thick and stamp out 2.5/3 cm rounds. (I use the bottom of a large piping nozzle for this). Knead and re-roll the leftovers until you have used all the pastry. Place the rounds on the baking tray and sprinkle with poppy seeds if using. Chill in the fridge for 10 minutes. Preheat the oven to 180 fan/200/gas 6.
3.   Bake the cheese bites 10–12 minutes until golden. Cool on a wire rack.

8. Index Recipe notes

Recipe notes

Unless specified otherwise I would use
Large eggs
Salted butter
Maldon sea salt flakes
Freshly ground black pepper
Bourneville chocolate
Vegetable bouillon powder
Unwaxed lemons
Good quality cocoa powder (do not substitute with hot chocolate powder)
Vanilla extract, not essence
Organic red lentils, they keep their shape better
Baking parchment for roasting vegetables will ensure that they do not stick and are easier to turn.
Good quality Italian tinned tomatoes for the best flavour
Baking parchment not greaseproof paper unless specified.
All recipes give approximate servings, but it will depend on your appetite!

Almonds
almond petit fours   193, **194**
whole orange and almond cake   158–59, **161**
Amy's chocolate brownies   170, **171**
apple and nut strudel   144
asparagus
pasta with asparagus, pea and mint pesto   62
warm asparagus and rocket salad with pesto dressing   35
aubergines Imam Bayıldı   45

Avocados
avocado and orange salad   **28**, 29
avocado and pistachio spaghetti   49
salmon fillets with avocado dressing   110, **111**

baked Alaska   147–48
baked mushrooms with sourdough toast   **97**, 99
Bakewell tart   138–39
basil and tomato risotto   47

Beans
butter bean purée   119
leek and cannellini bean soup   25
squash and green bean tagine   81
beef
beef with stout and pickled walnuts   124–25
lasagne   122, **123**
ragu   65–66
beetroot and orange pate   36, **37**
Bircher muesli   21, **23**
braised red cabbage with lentils and chorizo sausage   55–56
bread, wheaten   **23**, 24
brownies, Amy's chocolate   170, **171**
butter bean purée   119

buttermilk scones   188, **189**
butternut and goat's cheese tart   126–28, **127**

Cabbage
braised red cabbage with lentils and chorizo sausage   55–56

Cakes
Amy's chocolate brownies   170, **171**
Bakewell tart   138–39
carrot and walnut   172–73
chocolate cupcakes with chocolate frosting   174–75
chocolate fudge   176–78, **177**
chocolate roulade   149–50
lemon drizzle   179–80
Mars bar squares   185–86
mince pies   187
mincemeat and marzipan   181
walnut and mixed fruit   182–84, **183**
whole orange and almond   158–59, **161**
cannellini beans
leek and cannellini bean soup   25
carrot and walnut cake   172–73
casseroles
beef with stout and pickled walnuts   124–25
cauliflower cheese soufflés   100–101
cheese
butternut and goat's cheese tart   126–28, **127**
cheese bites   198, **199**
cheesy pasta bake   57
feta tarts   **86**, 87
goat's cheese parcels   88
goat's cheese soufflé   58–60, **59**
gorgonzola, chicory and fig salad   34
gorgonzola, chicory and walnut salad   33
marinated cheese and chilli salad   95
pear, watercress and Roquefort salad   32

roasted portabella mushrooms with spinach and taleggio   117
roasted vegetables with halloumi   51
taleggio risotto with walnut pesto   82
tomato and parmesan tart   85
twice baked cauliflower cheese soufflés   100–101
warm squash and lentil salad with halloumi   78, **79**
winter squash gratin   80
cheesecake, pear and amaretti   140–41

Chicken
chicken supreme   120–21
gingered chicken with noodles   50
chicory
gorgonzola, chicory and walnut salad   33

Chocolate
Amy's chocolate brownies   170, **171**
chocolate bites   **194**, 195
chocolate cupcakes with chocolate frosting   174–75
chocolate fudge cake   176–78, **177**
chocolate mousse   142, **143**
chocolate roulade   149–50
Ghirardelli Square chocolate ice cream   151
Mars bar squares   185–86
raspberry and white chocolate trifle   163–64
truffle torte   165

Chorizo sausage
braised red cabbage with lentils and chorizo sausage   55–56
chowder, creamy smoked haddock   77
confit, duck   105–6
creamy lamb curry   69–70, **73**
creamy smoked haddock chowder   77
cucumber raita   **73**, 74

Curries
creamy lamb   69–70, **73**
red lentil and sweet potato dhal   **73**, 75–76

duck confit   105–6

easy tomato sauce   42, **43**

Eggs
goat's cheese soufflé   58–60, **59**
twice baked cauliflower cheese soufflés   100–101

feta tarts   **86**, 87

Figs
gorgonzola, chicory and fig salad   34

Fish
creamy smoked haddock chowder   77
salmon fillets with avocado dressing   110, **111**

Ghirardelli Square chocolate ice cream   151
gingered chicken with noodles   50
gnocchi with tomato sauce   48

Goat's cheese
butternut and goat's cheese tart   126–28, **127**
goat's cheese parcels   88
goat's cheese soufflé   58–60, **59**
gorgonzola, chicory and fig salad   34
gorgonzola, chicory and walnut salad   33
granola   **19**, 20
green beans
squash and green bean tagine   81

Haddock
creamy smoked haddock chowder 77

Halloumi
roasted vegetables with halloumi 51
warm squash and lentil salad with halloumi 78, 79
hazelnut vacherin 135–36, **137**

ice cream, Ghirardelli Square chocolate 151
Irish soda bread **23**, 24

kedgeree 71
khichri 71–72, **73**

Lamb
creamy lamb curry 69–70, **73**
lamb and mint meatball tagine 114–15
slow-cooked leg of lamb 112–13
lasagne 122, **123**
lasagne, quick veggie 46
leek and cannellini bean soup 25
lemon drizzle cake 179–80
lemon posset 155
lemon syrup tart 156–57
lentils
braised red cabbage with lentils and chorizo sausage 55–56
khichri 71–72, **73**
red lentil and sweet potato dhal **73**, 75–76
red lentil pasta sauce 67
warm squash and lentil salad with halloumi 78, **79**

marinated cheese and chilli salad 95
marmalade, sweet Seville orange 22, **23**
Mars bar squares 185–86

Marzipan
mincemeat and marzipan cake   181

Meatballs
lamb and mint meatball tagine   114–15
meringue mice   190, **191**

Meringues
hazelnut vacherin   135–36, **137**
mince pies   187
mincemeat and marzipan cake   181
mousse, chocolate   142, **143**
muesli, Bircher   21, **23**

Mushrooms
baked mushrooms with sourdough toast   **97**, 99
mushroom samosas   **73**, 102–4, **103**
potato and mushroom risotto   64
roasted portabella   116–17

Noodles
gingered chicken with noodles   50
nougat   196–97

Oranges
avocado and orange salad   **28**, 29
beetroot and orange pate   36, **37**
orange Sauternes sauce   107
oranges in caramel   160, **161**
sweet Seville orange marmalade   22, **23**
whole orange and almond cake   158–59, **161**

pan haggerty   61

Pancetta
lasagne   122, **123**
ragu   65–66

Parmesan
tomato and parmesan tart   85

Pasta
with asparagus, pea and mint pesto   62
avocado and pistachio spaghetti   49
cheesy pasta bake   57
gnocchi with tomato sauce   48
lasagne   122, **123**
quick veggie lasagne   46
tarts' spaghetti   **43**, 44
with tomatoes and rocket   63

Pasta sauces
most useful easy tomato sauce   42, **43**
ragu   65–66
red lentil   67

Pastry
Bakewell tart   138–39
butternut and goat's cheese tart   126–28, **127**
feta tarts   **86**, 87
goat's cheese parcels   88
lemon syrup tart   156–57
mince pies   187
pea tart   83–84
pepper pissaladiere tartlets   129–30
roasted vegetable strudel   108–9
tomato and parmesan tart   85
pate, beetroot and orange   36, **37**

Pears
pear and amaretti cheesecake   140–41
pear, watercress and Roquefort salad   32

Peas
pasta with asparagus, pea and mint pesto   62
pea tart   83–84

Peppers
pepper pissaladiere tartlets   129–30
roasted red peppers   96, **97**

Pesto
pasta with asparagus, pea and mint pesto   62
taleggio risotto with walnut pesto   82
warm asparagus and rocket salad with pesto dressing   35
petit fours, almond   193, **194**

Pistachios
avocado and pistachio spaghetti   49

Pork
lasagne   122, **123**
ragu   65–66
portabella mushrooms, roasted   116–17
posset, lemon   155

Potatoes
pan haggerty   61
potato and mushroom risotto   64

Purées
butter bean   119
puttanesca pasta   **43**, 44

quick veggie lasagne   46

ragu   65–66
raita, cucumber   73, 74

Raspberries
raspberry and white chocolate trifle   163–64
shortbread and raspberry stacks   152–54, **153**

Red cabbage
braised red cabbage with lentils and chorizo sausage   55–56

Red lentils
red lentil and sweet potato dhal   **73**, 75–76
red lentil pasta sauce   67
red peppers, roasted   96, **97**

Rice
khichri   71–72, **73**
no-stir basil and tomato risotto   47
potato and mushroom risotto   64
taleggio risotto with walnut pesto   82

Risottos
no-stir basil and tomato   47
potato and mushroom   64
taleggio risotto with walnut pesto   82
roasted portabella mushrooms   116–17
roasted red peppers   96, **97**
roasted tomatoes   **97**, 98
roasted vegetable strudel   108–9
roasted vegetables with halloumi   51
roasted vegetables with sausages, horseradish sauce and baby Yorkshires   52–53

Rocket

warm asparagus and rocket salad with pesto dressing   35
romesco sauce   118

Roquefort

pear, watercress and Roquefort salad   32
roulade, chocolate   149–50

Salads

asparagus and rocket with pesto dressing   35
avocado and orange   **28**, 29
gorgonzola, chicory and fig   34
gorgonzola, chicory and walnut   33
hot tomato salad on sourdough toast   **30**, 31
marinated cheese and chilli   95
pear, watercress and Roquefort   32
warm squash and lentil salad with halloumi   78, **79**
salmon fillets with avocado dressing   110, **111**

Samosas

mushroom   **73**, 102–4, **103**

Sauces

orange Sauternes   107
romesco   118

Sausages

roasted vegetables with sausages, horseradish sauce and baby Yorkshires   52–53
scones, buttermilk   188, **189**
Seville orange marmalade   22, **23**
shortbread   **13**, 192
shortbread and raspberry stacks   152–54, **153**
slow-cooked leg of lamb   112–13
smoked haddock chowder   77
soda bread, Irish   **23**, 24

Soufflés
goat's cheese   58–60, **59**
twice baked cauliflower cheese   100–101

Soups
creamy smoked haddock chowder   77
leek and cannellini bean   25
squash and sweet potato   26
tomato   27

Sourdough
baked mushrooms with sourdough toast   **97**, 99
hot tomato salad on sourdough toast   **30**, 31

Spaghetti
avocado and pistachio   49
tarts'   **43**, 44
spiced tomatoes with naan bread   68

Spinach
roasted portabella mushrooms with spinach and taleggio   117

Squashes
butternut and goat's cheese tart   126–28, **127**
squash and green bean tagine   81
squash and sweet potato soup   26
warm squash and lentil salad with halloumi   78, **79**
winter squash gratin   80
sticky toffee puddings   145–46

Strudels
apple and nut   144
roasted vegetable   108–9

Sweet potatoes
red lentil and sweet potato dhal **73**, 75–76
squash and sweet potato soup 26

Tagines
lamb and mint meatball tagine 114–15
squash and green bean 81

Taleggio
roasted portabella mushrooms with spinach and taleggio 117
taleggio risotto with walnut pesto 82

Tarts
Bakewell 138–39
butternut and goats cheese 126–28, **127**
feta **86**, 87
lemon syrup 156–57
pea 83–84
pepper pissaladiere tartlets 129–30
tomato and parmesan 85
tarts' spaghetti **43**, 44
tiramisu 162

Tomatoes
gnocchi with tomato sauce 48
hot tomato salad on sourdough toast 30, 31
most useful easy tomato sauce 42, 43
no-stir basil and tomato risotto 47
pasta with tomatoes and rocket 63
roasted tomatoes 97, 98
spiced tomatoes with naan bread 68
tomato and parmesan tart 85
tomato soup 27
trifle, raspberry and white chocolate 163–64
truffle torte 165

vacherin, hazelnut   135–36, 137

Vegetables
roasted vegetable strudel   108–9
roasted vegetables with halloumi   51
roasted vegetables with sausages, horseradish sauce and baby Yorkshires   52–53
veggie lasagne   46

Walnuts
beef with stout and pickled walnuts   124–25
carrot and walnut cake   172–73
gorgonzola, chicory and walnut salad   33
taleggio risotto with walnut pesto   82
walnut and mixed fruit cake   182–84, **183**

Watercress
pear, watercress and Roquefort salad   32
wheaten bread   **23**, 24
whole orange and almond cake   158–59, **161**
winter squash gratin   80